quot	quotation marks improperly placed in relation to punctuation mark **45, 46, 47**
ref	faulty pronoun reference **16**
rep	careless repetition **26**
restr	punctuate a restrictive clause properly **40**
sp	spelling error
title	improper format of title for published work **48, 49**
trite	trite expression **30**
vb	improper form of verb **17**
wdy	wordy sentence **21**
ww	wrong word **28**

Proofreaders' Marks

⌒	close up space
ℓ	delete
℮	delete and close up space
#	separate with a space
∧	insert here what is indicated in the margin
¶	start new paragraph
no ¶	no paragraph; run in with previous paragraph
⊙/	insert period
⋀/	insert comma
;/	insert semicolon
:/	insert colon
⌐ᴍ/	insert em dash
ᴍ/ ᴍ	insert pair of em dashes
=/	insert hyphen
∨/	insert apostrophe
cap	use capital letter here
lc	use lowercase letter here
ital	set in italic type
rom	set in roman type
sc	set in small capitals
bf	set in boldface type
tr	transpose letters or words

The Little English Handbook

Eighth Edition

Edward **P. J.** Corbett
The Ohio State University

Sheryl **L.** Finkle
North Central College

 LONGMAN

An Imprint of Addison Wesley Longman

New York • Reading, Massachusetts • Menlo Park, California • Harlow, England
Don Mills, Ontario • Sydney • Mexico City • Madrid • Amsterdam

Publishing Partner: Anne Smith
Assistant Editor: Karen Helfrich
Production Manager: Valerie A. Sawyer
Desktop Administration: Jim Sullivan
Manufacturing Manager: Hilda Koparanian
Electronic Page Makeup: Jim Sullivan
Printer and Binder: RR Donnelley & Sons Company
Cover Printer: Phoenix Color Corp.

Library of Congress Cataloging-in-Publication Data

Corbett, Edward P. J.
    The little English handbook : choices and conventions / Edward
P. J. Corbett, Sheryl L. Finkle.—8th ed.
        p.   cm.
    Includes index.
    ISBN: 0-321-04965-9
        1. English language—Rhetoric—Handbooks, manuals, etc.
    2. English language—Usage—Handbooks, manuals, etc. I. Finkle,
Sheryl L. II. Title
PE1408.C587   1997
808'.042—DC21   97-9865
                                                              CIP

ISBN: 0-321-04965-9

678910-DOC-03

This book is dedicated to all our students over the years, whose written prose sometimes mystified us, often enlightened us, and invariably beguiled us. Bless them all.

Contents

PREFACE

The Little English Handbook is designed to serve as a guide on basic matters of grammar, style, paragraphing, punctuation, and mechanics for those engaged in writing public prose. By *public prose* we mean that dialect of written English most commonly used in the newspapers, magazines, and books that the majority of educated English speakers read. This dialect ranges in style from the formal to the casual, from the literary to the colloquial. But because public prose has to be intelligible to a general audience, it avoids the esoteric vocabulary of various professional, regional, and social groups, and it observes the rules of grammar as taught in the schools.

The use of the term *public prose* is not intended to disparage the other current dialects, most of which serve well the needs of some of the people all of the time and all of the people some of the time. Obviously, spoken English, with its own wide range of professional, regional, and social dialects, serves the needs of more people more often than written English does. However, despite the primacy of the spoken language, there are occasions when many, if not most, English speakers must use the written language in order to record or communicate their thoughts, needs, and feelings. It is for those occasions that this handbook was prepared.

A Handbook for Common Problems

Ever since the first edition of this handbook, we have concentrated on those matters of grammar, style, paragraphing, punctuation, and mechanics that, from years of experience in reading students' papers and responding to telephone queries from people in business and the professions, we know to be the most common and persistent problems in the expressive part of the writing process. For answers to the larger and more subtle problems in writing prose, you will have to consult one of the larger handbooks. We do not, for instance, provide guidance in all the uses of the comma; some of those uses are never or only seldom a problem for writers. Instead, we deal only with those half-dozen conventions of the comma that are most often ignored or misused and that are most crucial for the preservation of clarity. If you master these six uses, you can rest assured that you can make no really serious mistakes in the use (or the omission) of the comma.

Choices and Conventions

The subtitle of this handbook, *Choices and Conventions*, reflects our approach. Some of the principles governing the system of writing have been established by conventions; others represent recommendations from a number of options. Accordingly, in most cases, we have stated the guiding principle in definite, unequivocal terms. We are the first to concede, however, that in matters of language, there should be no absolute prescriptions or proscriptions. Where choices are available, you must be guided in making your selection by a consideration of the subject matter, the occasion, the desired effect, and your audience. But in our experience, those who need the guidance of a handbook want a simple, straightforward answer to their query.

Priorities in the Writing Process

By concentrating on matters of grammar, style, paragraphing, punctuation, and mechanics, we do not wish to imply that these are the most important concerns of "good writing." What is most necessary for effective communication is the substance, originality, and sophistication of your thoughts and your ability to organize your thoughts in a unified, coherent way. Inept articulation of your thoughts is often a reflection of inept processes of invention and organization.

Careless expression stems, ultimately, from careless thinking. Observance of the "basics" treated in this handbook will not guarantee that your prose will be interesting to read or worth reading, but observance of the fundamental conventions of the writing system will at least guarantee that your prose *can* be read. Readable prose is no mean achievement. The next achievement to strive for is to write prose that others will *want* to read.

Changes in the Eighth Edition

Sheryl L. Finkle has made the most significant contribution to this eighth edition of *LEH*. She has reorganized and rewritten many of the sections in four of our major divisions—those on grammar, style, paragraphing, and punctuation and mechanics—in order to make these sections more accessible to those students who did not adequately absorb the instruction they may have had in grammar and composition in grade school and high school. She has also added several new faulty student sentences supplied by her former colleague at Ohio State University, Cheryl Dobroka. Edward P. J. Corbett is responsible for the changes made in the second half of the book—the sections on the research paper, the forms of letters, the glossary of usage, and the glossary of grammatical terms. The most significant change he has made in the section on the research paper is the addition of two more documentation systems, the ACW system (Alliance for Computers and Writing) and the footnote system presented in *The Chicago Manual of Style.* Two new papers have been added as specimens of the MLA (Modern Language Association) system and the APA (American Psychological Association) system, and we have retained the display of the CBE (Council of Biology Editors) documentation system. And in the glossary of grammatical terms, we have retained the terms that Professor Jocelyn Steer supplied for our seventh edition, terms that will be of special help to students of English as a second language (ESL). Entries in this glossary that pose significant problems for ESL students are highlighted in color for easy reference.

Acknowledgments

Every textbook designed for classroom use profits from criticisms and suggestions of experienced, knowledgeable teachers. The list of teachers who reviewed the manuscript of the first edition, who provided detailed critiques of subsequent editions, and who buttonholed us at conventions to offer their suggestions for improving the text would be a long one indeed. We resort here to a collective word of appreciation to those teachers whose suggestions greatly improved previous editions. But we do want to acknowledge by name the teachers who were commissioned to review the seventh edition of the book and the manuscript of the eighth edition and provided helpful suggestions:

Barry Alford, Mid Michigan Community College
Randall Mann, University of Florida
Anthony P. Petruzzi, University of Nebraska
James M. Wallace, University of Akron

The authors of any textbook also owe a great debt of gratitude to many people on the staff of their publisher—not only the people in the editorial department but also the people in the design, the production, and the marketing departments. If we were to acknowledge by name all those on the staff of Longman to whom we are indebted, the list would extend for several more inches. But we want to single out for special mention here a few people who have been involved in the preparation and production of this edition of *The Little English Handbook*: Anne Smith, Karen Helfrich, Leslie Taggart, and Marina Vaynshteyn.

EDWARD P. J. CORBETT
SHERYL L. FINKLE

Legend

Some of the conventions presented in this handbook, especially those having to do with punctuation, are illustrated with graphic models using these symbols:

⬚ = word

A word inside the box designates a particular part of speech, e.g., noun.

_____ = phrase

A phrase is a meaningful combination of two or more words that does not constitute a clause.

The following abbreviations on the horizontal line designate a particular kind of phrase, e.g., 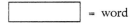prep.

prep. = prepositional phrase (**on the bus**)
part. = participial phrase (**having ridden on the bus**)
ger. = gerund phrase (**riding on the bus** pleased him)
inf. = infinitive phrase (he wanted **to ride on the bus**)

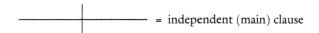 = independent (main) clause

An independent clause, sometimes referred to as a *main clause,* can stand by itself as a grammatically complete sentence, e.g., **He rode on the bus.** The vertical line indicates the separation of subject from predicate.

1

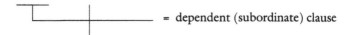 = dependent (subordinate) clause

A dependent clause, sometimes referred to as a *subordinate clause,* cannot stand by itself as a grammatically complete sentence.

The following abbreviations printed above the first vertical line designate a particular kind of dependent clause, e.g.,

noun = noun clause (He claimed **that he rode on the bus.**)

adj. = adjective clause (The man **who rode on the bus** was pleased.)

adv. = adverb clause (He was late **because he rode on the bus.**)

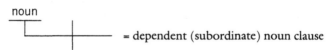 = dependent (subordinate) noun clause

Format of Manuscript

Most editors or instructors provide directions about the format for the final copy of your writing. However, if no specific directions are given, you can be confident that the format of your manuscript will be acceptable if you observe the following conventions.

1 Write on one side of the paper only.

2 Double-space the lines of prose, whether you handwrite or typewrite.

A manuscript submitted to an editor for consideration must be typewritten and double-spaced.

3 Preserve a left-hand and a right-hand margin.

4 Put the title of your paper at the top of the first page of your manuscript—even though you may have put the title on a cover sheet.

5 Number all pages at the top of the page—in the middle or at the right-hand margin.

6 Secure your manuscript with a paper clip.

Many editors will not even read a manuscript that is stapled together.

7 Use the proper kind of paper.

If you typewrite your manuscript, use white, unlined, opaque paper. If you handwrite your manuscript, use white, lined theme paper.

Clear, Effective Paragraphs

One way to regard paragraphing is to view it as a system of marking stages of thought presented in units larger than the word and the sentence. When writers revise and then edit a piece of writing, they often begin by reviewing the overall substance and strategy of the piece (or the thinking in and among paragraphs) because decisions that are made at this global level of review have a strong impact on local decisions made about sentence structure and word choice. If writers first labor to edit each sentence in a piece of writing for grammatical soundness and then decide that half of those sentences need to be struck from a paragraph entirely or need to be moved and reshaped to fit the context of other paragraphs, they run the risk of having to repeat the initial editing efforts one or more times, expending not only time but energy and patience as well. With these concerns in mind, we address the revision of paragraphs before the revision and editing of sentences and words.

Paragraphing is a graphic means of alerting readers to a shift of focus in the development of the main idea of the whole discourse. It marks off for the reader's convenience the individually distinct but related parts of the whole discourse, much as pauses and shifts in the tone of a speaker's voice (more unconsciously) signal movement or change in a stream of connected oral discourse.

The typographical device most commonly used to mark off written paragraphs is **indentation.** The first line of each new paragraph starts several spaces (usually five spaces) from the left-hand margin. However, certain forms of writing, like the single-spaced, typewritten business letter, regularly use an alternative convention called the **block system** for marking paragraphs. In this system, the writer begins the first line of the paragraph at the left-hand margin, leaving double or triple spaces between paragraphs. *How do we know where to mark off paragraphs and how to develop and organize sentences within these boundaries?* Any good writing text will illustrate the common patterns of paragraph development. Here we focus on creating **unity, completeness,** and **coherence,** in and among paragraphs because these are the areas of paragraph construction where writers need the most assistance in the revision and editing stages of writing.

8

8 Developing a Single Topic (Unity)

Preserve the unity of the paragraph.

A paragraph should develop a single topic or thesis, which is often—but not always—announced in a topic sentence. Every sentence in the paragraph should contribute in some way to the development of this topic. When writers introduce other ideas into the paragraph, they disrupt the unity of the paragraph and disorient their readers.

Sample revisions:

> **Original:** Priests are still in great demand today because of the rapid increase of population in the United States and in other parts of the world. The Catholic Church is losing many possible followers because it does not have enough "teachers" to guide those who want to become part of some religion. The Pope has been very adamant about keeping the laws that have existed for centuries. These laws prohibit the ordination of married men. The times have changed, and the job that once was held in high esteem is now in search of applicants. The Catholic Church needs to reconsider some of its outmoded laws.

One possible revision: The rapid increase of population throughout the world has created a great demand for priests, but the supply of priests has declined dramatically in the last fifty years or so. Consequently, the Catholic Church has been losing many potential followers because it does not have enough "teachers" to guide those who want to become part of some religion. One reason for the marked decline in the number of applicants for the priesthood is that the Pope is very adamant about keeping the age-old laws that prohibit the ordination of married men. The inadequate supply of priests will probably persist as long as the Church refuses to reconsider these outmoded laws.

8

Explanation:

The original paragraph about priests has a certain unity: each sentence is saying something about the desperate need for more Catholic priests to serve the growing population. But it is difficult to discern the thread that stitches all of the sentences into a unit. If the first sentence is the intended topic sentence, the paragraph would have to take on a different shape from the one in the original. But since most of the sentences are talking about the causes of the current shortage of priests, it seems likely that the intended topic of the paragraph is implicit in a combination of the first and second sentences. We gave this paragraph some unity by devising a topic sentence that could serve as an umbrella for all of the other sentences in the paragraph.

Original: Dr. Rockwell let his feelings be known on only one subject: the administration. He felt the administrative system was outdated. Abolishing grades, giving students a voice in the administration, and revamping the curriculum were three steps he felt should be taken to improve the system. Dr. Rockwell taught in this manner. In class, a mysterious aura surrounded him. He was "hip" to what was going on, but he preferred to listen to the members of his class rather than himself. He was quiet and somewhat shy. His eyes caught everything that went on in his class. His eyes generated a feeling of understanding.

One possible revision: Dr. Rockwell let his feelings be known on only one subject: the administration. His estimation of the administrative system of the school was largely negative. He felt, for instance, that the administrative system was outdated. Abolishing grades, giving students a voice in the administration, and revamping the curriculum were three steps he felt should be taken to improve the system.

8

Dr. Rockwell's demeanor in the classroom was remarkable. Although there was a mysterious aura about him, he was always "hip" to what was going on. His eyes caught everything that went on in his class, but they generated a feeling of understanding. Even though he was a learned scholar, this quiet, somewhat shy man preferred to listen to the members of his class rather than himself.

Explanation:

Like the paragraph about the priests, the paragraph about Dr. Rockwell has a certain unity: each sentence in the paragraph is talking about the teacher Dr. Rockwell. And there is a tight unity about the first three sentences: each of these sentences talks about Dr. Rockwell's attitude toward the administration. But with the fourth sentence of the paragraph, the writer introduces another and unrelated topic: a description of how Dr. Rockwell conducted himself in the classroom. We broke up this stretch of prose into two paragraphs and reorganized some of the sentences so that each of the two paragraphs would have its own unity.

A paragraph will have unity—will have "oneness"—if every sentence in it has an obvious bearing on the development of a single topic. When writers sense that they have shifted to the discussion of another topic, they should begin a new paragraph.

9 Developing Ideas Fully (Completeness)

Paragraphs should be adequately developed.

Judgment about whether a paragraph is adequately developed is, of course, a relative matter. Because some ideas need more development than others, no one can say, in the abstract, how many sentences a paragraph needs in order to be adequately developed. Each paragraph must be judged on its own terms and in the context in which it appears. If a paragraph has a topic sentence, for instance, that topic sentence can dictate how long the paragraph needs to be. What was done in a previous paragraph and what will be done in a paragraph that follows may dictate how long the middle paragraph should be.

The first step in developing a paragraph is to consider its central idea—whether that is expressed in a topic sentence or is merely implied—and to determine what that idea commits you to doing. Asking yourself a series of questions about what you are trying to say and do in successive sentences of your original paragraph will help you to make a choice of the appropriate means of developing or extending your thinking in that paragraph. Here is a list of the common ways in which writers develop their paragraphs.

Common Means Writers Use to Develop Paragraphs

1. They present examples or illustrations of what they are discussing.
2. They cite data—facts, statistics, evidence, details, and precedents—that corroborate or confirm what they are discussing.
3. They quote, paraphrase, or summarize the testimony of others about what they are discussing.

4. They relate an anecdote or event that has some bearing on what they are discussing.
5. They define terms connected with what they are discussing.
6. They compare or contrast what they are discussing with something else—usually something familiar to the reader.
7. They explore the causes or reasons for the phenomenon or situation they are discussing.
8. They point out the effects or consequences of the phenomenon or situation they are discussing.
9. They explain how something operates.
10. They describe the person, place, or thing they are discussing.

9

Sample revisions:

Original: Corporations make frequent use of group conversation in order to develop communication among their employees. The effectiveness of this technique is one of the keys to successful communication between management and workers.

One possible revision: The effectiveness of group conversation is one of the keys to successful communication between management and workers in many corporations. It is not sufficient that the opportunity for group conversation be set up. Those who conduct such sessions must make sure that everyone in the group makes a contribution to the conversation. And workers must not be intimidated by managers. Managers, for their part, must be willing to tolerate workers' disagreement with their views. The greater the liveliness and the heatedness of the conversation, the greater the chance that a favorable climate for real communication will be established. Genuine communication among the employees enhances amity and productivity.

Explanation:

This sample paragraph and its revision have been taken out of context, but even so, we can sense the inadequate development of the skimpy original paragraph. It raises some expectations that are not satisfied. The first sentence mentions that some corporations make frequent use of group conversation as a means of developing communication among their employees. If what preceded this paragraph did not define what "group conversation" is, we would expect this paragraph to give us that explanation. If the previous paragraph did define "group conversation," the first sentence of this paragraph would lead us to expect some evidence or examples to be given of the use of group conversations by corporations or to expect some discussion of how group conversations improve communication among employees. Instead, the second sentence of the paragraph raises yet another set of expectations for readers: show us *how* this technique proves to be the key to successful communication between management and workers. The writer of this paragraph has to decide what the topic of the paragraph will be and then must develop that topic sufficiently in the rest of the paragraph. We have developed this paragraph by showing how group conversation fosters communication.

Original: My position on animal research is a combination of the views of the researchers and the activists. The best way to proceed is with caution and balance between compassion and compelling reasons to conduct research. We need to enhance life but not destroy someone else's if possible. This view seems to be a moderate one in the scheme of people's thinking.

One possible revision: My own position on animal research combines the concerns of both researchers and activists. Like the researchers, I believe that there are compelling reasons to continue to explore cures for deadly diseases, improved surgical procedures, benefits of medicines, and even transplants. These treatments are a matter of life and death for all species. Think about how much pain, suffering, and death a cure for cancer could eliminate. But I also believe that we need to be compassionate toward other species. If experiments are particularly cruel, prolonged, and painful, we should do all we can to find alternative methods of study, like computer simulations, even when they are slower or less effective. Animal testing should be a last resort for medical testing. Cosmetic product-testing and other "incidental" uses of animal life can be avoided completely if we simply choose to value life itself above certain life-enhancement choices.

9

Explanation:

The original paragraph about the student's views on animal research presents a number of generalized ideas but does not provide specific details to support the generalities. After responding to several questions about what certain words she has used mean (*compassionate, compelling*), what the researchers and activists she cites have said, and what consequences or benefits the various experiments offer, the student was able to revise her paragraph to provide her readers with a better idea of what conditions for experimentation she supports and where she draws the line on conducting animal research.

In the two examples above, we have illustrated how to use some of the common means of developing paragraphs to revise inadequately developed prose. The revisions are only one of several ways that these writers could have reworked their prose. In each case, however, the writers were able to consider the different ways of developing paragraphs, pose some questions to themselves using those common means of development, and then incorporate their responses to those questions into their writing to help their readers understand more fully what they were trying to say.

Deliberate use of one- or two-sentence paragraphs:

Generally, one- and two-sentence paragraphs are not justifiable, except for purposes of emphasis, transition, or dialogue.

Use of one- or two-sentence paragraphs for emphasis:

Note that the previous sentence is also a paragraph, justifiable in its use on the grounds that the writers wanted to give special emphasis to a principle by setting it aside in a paragraph by itself. Emphasizing a word or phrase by putting it in a separate paragraph is comparable to emphasizing a word or phrase in a sentence by underlining or italicizing it. Set aside in a paragraph by itself, an important idea achieves a prominence that would be missed if the idea were merged with other ideas in the same paragraph.

9

Use of one- or two-sentence paragraphs to create transition:

A one- or two-sentence paragraph can also be used to mark or signal a transition from one major division of a discourse to the next major division. These transitional paragraphs facilitate reading because they orient readers, reminding them of what has been discussed and alerting them to what is going to be discussed. Such paragraphs are like signposts marking the major stages of a journey. Note how the following two-sentence transitional paragraph looks backward to what has been discussed and forward to what will be discussed:

> After presenting his introduction to *Songs of Experience*, William Blake apparently feels that his readers have been sufficiently warned about their earthly predicament. Let us see now how he uses the poems in *Songs of Experience* to illustrate what the people might do to solve their problems.

Paragraphing dialogue:

One of the conventions of printing is that, in representing dialogue in a story, we should begin a new paragraph every time the speaker changes. A paragraph of dialogue can be one sentence long or ten sentences long (any number of sentences, in fact). A paragraph of dialogue may also consist of only a phrase or a single word. Note the paragraphing of the following stretch of dialogue:

> "Look at that cloudless blue sky," Melvin said. "There doesn't seem to be any bottom to that blue. It's beautiful, isn't it?"
>
> "Yup," Hank muttered.
>
> "Remember yesterday?"
>
> "Yup."
>
> "I thought it would never stop raining."
>
> "Me too."

10

Once an exchange like that gets going, the author can dispense with the identifying tags, because each separate paragraph will mark the shift in speaker.

Except for the purposes of emphasis, transition, or dialogue, a one- or two-sentence paragraph can rarely be justified. One sentence is hardly enough to qualify as both the topic sentence and the development of the idea posed by that topic sentence.

10 Making Ideas Easy to Follow (Coherence)

Compose the paragraph so that it reads coherently.

Coherence is the quality that makes it easy for a reader to follow a writer's train of thought from sentence to sentence and from paragraph to paragraph. Coherence facilitates reading because it ensures that the reader will be able to detect the relationship of the parts of a discourse. It also reflects clear thinking by the writer because it results from the writer's arrangement of ideas in some kind of perceptible order and from the writer's use of those verbal devices that help stitch thoughts together. In short, as the Latin roots of the word suggest (*co*, "together," plus *haerere*, "to stick"), coherence helps the parts of a discourse to "stick together."

10

Ways to Achieve Coherence in a Paragraph

1. Repeat key words from sentence to sentence or use recognizable synonyms for key words.
2. Use pronouns for key nouns. (Because a pronoun gets its meaning from the noun to which it refers, it is by its very nature one of those devices that helps to stitch sentences together.)
3. Use demonstrative adjectives, which are "pointing words" (e.g., **this** statement, **that** plan, **these** developments, **those** disasters).
4. Use conjunctive adverbs, which are "thought-connecting words" (e.g., **however, moreover, also, nevertheless, therefore, thus, subsequently, indeed, then, accordingly**).
5. Arrange the sequence of sentences in some kind of perceptible order (e.g., a **time order,** as in a narrative of what happened or in an explanation of how to do something; a **space order,** as in the description of a physical object or a scene; a **logical order,** such as cause to effect, effect to cause, general to particular, particular to general, whole to part, familiar to unfamiliar).

Here are some examples of incoherent paragraphs and revisions based on the suggested ways to achieve coherence.

Original: Construction on Interstate 71 near downtown Columbus and north of that area will begin this fall. Traffic backups need to be prevented by an alternative north and south detour that will be mapped out by this office. Congestion needs to be alleviated, and potentially dangerous situations need to be avoided. A detour will prevent traffic backups that occur if one-lane traffic is permitted. An alternative is important because of the high-density flow of traffic during peak commuting hours.

Revision: Construction on Interstate 71 near downtown Columbus and north of that area will begin this fall. Therefore, our office needs to plan a detour for north-south traffic in order to alleviate congestion and avoid potentially dangerous situations. Specifically, this detour must reduce the traffic backups that occur when one-lane flow is permitted on the highway during construction. The alternate route that our office will map out is a particularly effective way to remedy the situation because of the high-density flow of traffic on this route, especially during peak commuting hours.

10

Explanation:

In this paragraph about constructing a detour for Interstate 71, the writer provides several pieces of information about the constraints on and importance of constructing an alternative traffic route. However, it is difficult to understand the relationship among these different pieces of information. By using demonstrative adjectives (**this detour**), conjunctive adverbs (**therefore** and **specifically**), repeating key words, and arranging the sequences of words in logical order, we have developed one way to help the reader understand better what needs to be accomplished and why it is important.

Original: As a young athlete, I played many sports, and baseball was my favorite. I never wanted to stop playing the game. I wanted to become a professional athlete like Willie Stargell or Roberto Clemente. During the time I played, the people who coached me were major influences on me both on and off the field. The coaches would teach me and give me tips to improve my baseball skills and techniques. My coaches taught me discipline and respect, which I use in everyday situations. After my time as a baseball player was over, I continued to be a fan of the game. I watched baseball and softball games as much as I could. As I watched the games, I noticed a lack of knowledge and ability on the part of some coaches. The lack of knowledge and ability bothered me because these coaches were not able to bring out the potential of the young athletes. Young athletes between the ages of eight and twelve are very impressionable, and they need role models who can influence them for the rest of their lives.

10

Revision: As a young athlete, I played many sports, but baseball was my favorite. I liked baseball so much that I wanted to become a professional athlete like Willie Stargell or Roberto Clemente. During the time I played baseball, my coaches had a great influence on my development both on and off the field. On the field, my coaches helped me improve my skills as an athlete. Off the field, too, they taught me discipline and respect, which I still use in everyday situations in my professional life. My coaches' influence was so great that even after I stopped being an active player, I continued to watch baseball and softball games. But one thing I noticed as I watched these games was the lack of knowledge and skills manifested by the coaches today. Because of their ineptness, these coaches were not able to bring out the potential of the young athletes by developing the players' skills as my coaches had been able to develop my skills. More disappointing, because they were not good role models, cultivating the kind of discipline and respect my own coaches had emphasized, they did not seem to be able to influence their highly impressionable young athletes, as I was influenced, for the rest of their lives.

Explanation:

This writer has set an ambitious task for himself. He attempts to use personal narrative to critique coaching. Thus, he has to juggle both time and logical order in the development of the paragraph. He discusses how he learned to love baseball so much that he wanted to become a professional player, how he developed sound baseball skills from his coaches, and how he learned discipline and respect through his coaches' influence. The writer begins to have difficulty midway through the paragraph when he attempts to contrast the experiences of youngsters today with his own experiences. We can sense that the writer believes that current coaches are not providing as worthwhile an experience for their players as the writer's own coaches had. Still, the writer is vague in how he recounts the relationship of the coaches' knowledge to their ability to bring out potential in young people and their ability to serve as effective role models. On first glance, it is difficult to suggest ways to revise this paragraph because it is difficult to determine the writer's central message. The best way to develop a sense of the message is to confer with the writer, "saying back" what we took away from the text as we read and discussing with the writer how close we came to his desired message and effect. After this kind of initial consultation with the writer, we asked him to clarify his thinking in terms of the two kinds of order he was trying to establish: time order and logical order. The writer sketched out both the time frames he wanted to represent *(his playing time and his viewing time)* and the issues he wanted to compare and contrast in his playing time and in his viewing time *(teaching skills and influencing behavior through discipline and respect)*. Working from this sketch, we helped the writer revise this paragraph by asking a series of questions about what he had learned, when, from whom, and how. Then, to revise the paragraph, the writer used some key repeating words, some connecting words, and a new frame for arranging his sentences.

Coherence is a difficult writing skill to master, but as you develop more skill in this area, you will find it easier to communicate with others on paper. Consciously identify what words will make the sequence of thought flow smoothly, easily, and logically from sentence to sentence and help readers to pass from sentence to sentence without being puzzled about the relationship of what is said in one sentence to what is said in another.

Grammatical Sentences

Grammar may be defined as the study of how a language "works"—a study of how the structural system of a language combines with a vocabulary to convey meaning. When we study a foreign language, we study both vocabulary and grammar because, until we can put the two together, we cannot bring meaning to language. Considerations of both vocabulary and grammar are important to us as writers and readers of our own language for the same reasons. When we know the grammar of a sentence but not the meaning of each individual word, it can be difficult to make sense of the sentence. Consider the following word sequence:

> The porturbs in the brigger torms have tanted the maret's rotment brokly.

Although most of the words in that sequence are unfamiliar, you can sense that the sequence has the structure of the kind of English sentence that makes a statement. You might further guess that this statement pattern is one that says *porturbs* (whoever they are) have done something to *rotment* (whatever that is); or to put it another way, that *porturbs* is the subject of the sentence, that *have tanted* is the predicate verb, and that *rotment* is the object of that verb, the receiver of action performed by the doer, *porturbs*. The more words you know in the sentence, the more easily you can figure out the unfamiliar vocabulary from contextual clues or by a dictionary check.

Now, consider the problem of meaning-making in the following sentence:

> Becoming to successful deterrent executions would have a high rate enough to put thought in the back of the would-be killers pulling the trigger they would pull the trigger on their lives.

In this instance, even though you may know the meaning of every word in the sentence, it is difficult to bring meaning to this sequence of words because you need to work very hard to identify the function of the words and the logical structure or grammar of the sequence.

This section of the handbook deals with those devices that make it possible for written sentences to convey a writer's intended meaning clearly to a reader. Although most problems with grammar are not as extreme or obvious as the case we have just presented, they can be difficult for you to identify as you are writing and revising your own discourse. Thus, offering your work to a peer reader or reading the writing yourself in ways that deliberately expose potential problems in the following areas can be helpful.

Many of the technical terms used in the grammar section—and in later sections—are defined when the term is first used, and they may also be defined in the glossary of grammatical terms at the back of the handbook.

11 Complete Sentences (Fragments)

Complete sentences are a convention of most writing communities, even though in some instances writers may use sentences that do not look complete or writers may intentionally use sentence fragments for stylistic effect. An effective writer exercises control over sentence boundaries to maximize a reader's attention, acceptance, and comprehension.

A sentence fragment is the opposite of a complete sentence. It is a string of words appearing between an initial capital letter and a final period or question mark, that does one of the following: lacks a subject or a finite-verb predicate (or both); has a subject and a finite-verb predicate but is made part of a larger structure by a relative pronoun (**who, which, that**) or by a subordinating conjunction (**although, because, if, when**). According to that definition, all four of the strings of words in boldface below qualify as sentence fragments.

Identifying Complete Sentences

In order to be considered complete, a sentence must

- have a subject (stated or implied).
- have a verb.
- *not* begin with a subordinating word which signals dependence on another set of words to complete a thought.

11

Sample revisions:

Original (1): They tried to console the mother for the tragic death of her son. **Although they soon realized that no words they could utter would comfort her.**

Revision: They tried to console the mother for the tragic death of her son, although they soon realized that no words they could utter would comfort her.

Original (2): The reason for Holden's disappointment being that his sister wasn't there to comfort him.

Possible revisions: The reason for Holden's disappointment was that his sister wasn't there to comfort him.

or

Holden was disappointed because his sister was not there to comfort him.

Original (3): Seniors need to preregister early to prevent being closed out of their courses. **Courses that they need in order to qualify for graduation in June.**

Revision: Seniors need to preregister early to prevent being closed out of required courses that they need to qualify for graduation in June.

Original (4): Before enrolling for professors' elective courses, students should gather as much information as they can. **The professors' grading policies, the number of papers they assign during the semester, the kinds of examination they give, and attendance policies.**

Revision: Before enrolling in elective courses, students should gather as much information as they can: the professors' grading policies, the number of papers they assign during the semester, the kinds of examination they give, and their attendance policies.

11

Explanation:

In the passages above, we have revised sentence fragments to create complete constructions that help the reader to understand relationships among ideas more clearly. For instance, in sentence 1, the string of words beginning with **although** and terminating with a period is a sentence fragment because, even though it has a subject (**they**) and a finite-verb predicate (**realized**), it is turned into a dependent clause by the subordinating conjunction **although.** If, instead of using the subordinating conjunction **although,** the writer had used a coordinating conjunction (**but**) or a conjunction adverb (**however**) to begin that clause, the string of words would be a complete sentence. If **although** is used to begin the string of words, however, that string must be made part of the preceding independent clause.

The string of words in sentence 2 and the second string of words in sentence 3 are sentence fragments. Although sentence 2 has a verbal in it (**being**), that participle by itself cannot constitute the predicate of an independent clause. Note that we made this string of words a complete sentence simply by substituting the finite verb **was** for the participle **being.** Sentence 3 has a finite verb, **need,** but that verb is the predicate of the dependent adjective clause beginning with **that.**

The second string of words in sentence 4 has two finite verbs in it (**assign** and **give**), but both of these verbs serve as the predicate of dependent adjective clauses (**papers [that] they assign, kinds of ex-**

aminations [that] they give). Note that we have joined that predi-
cateless string of words to the previous independent clause by re-
placing the period with a colon and by reducing the capital letter in
The to a lowercase **t**. As a result of the revision, the two strings of
words stand as a single complete sentence.

Whether a string of words constitutes a complete sentence or
only a sentence fragment is a grammatical concern; whether the use
of a sentence fragment is appropriate in a particular context is a
rhetorical or stylistic concern. It is a fact of life that we sometimes
communicate with one another in sentence fragments. Note for instance the following exchange:

> Where are you going tonight?
> The movies.
> Who with?
> Jack.
> Where?
> The Palace.
> What time?
> About 8:30.
> By car?
> No, by bus.
> Can I go?
> Sure.

Once the context of that dialogue was established, both speakers
communicated in fragmentary sentences. Notice, however, that the
dialogue had to be initiated by a complete sentence (the question
Where are you going tonight?) and that, later, the first speaker had
to resort again to a complete sentence (**Can I go?**) because there was
no way to phrase that question clearly in a fragment.

Native speakers of a language can converse in fragments because
each of them is capable of mentally supplying what is missing from an
utterance. When in response to the initial questions the second
speaker answers, **The movies,** that phrase conveys a meaning because

the first speaker is able to supply, mentally, the missing elements in the fragmentary reply: **[I am going to] the movies.**

All of us have encountered sentence fragments in the written prose of some very reputable writers. Sentences without verbs are most likely to be found in mood-setting descriptive and narrative prose, as in this first paragraph of Charles Dickens's novel *Bleak House:*

> London, Michaelmas Term lately over, and the Lord Chancellor sitting in Lincoln's Inn Hall. Implacable November weather. As much mud in the streets, as if the waters had but newly retired from the face of the earth, and it would not be wonderful to meet a Megalosaurus, forty feet long or so, waddling like an elephantine lizard up Holborn Hill. Smoke lowering down from chimney-pots, making a soft black drizzle, with flakes of soot in it as big as full-grown snow-flakes—gone into mourning, one might imagine, for the death of the sun. Dogs, undistinguishable in mire. Horses, scarcely better; splashed to their blinkers. Foot passengers, jostling one another's umbrellas, in a general infection of ill-temper, and losing their foothold at street-corners, where tens of thousands of other foot passengers have been slipping and sliding since the day broke (if this day ever broke), adding new deposits to the crust upon crust of mud, sticking at those points tenaciously to the pavement and accumulating at compound interest.

In this paragraph, there are a few clauses (that is, groups of words with a subject and a finite-verb predicate), but the paragraph consists primarily of nouns and noun phrases, some of them modified by participial phrases (e.g., **sitting in Lincoln's Inn Hall, splashed to their blinkers, jostling one another's umbrellas**). Although the passage is largely lacking in statements made with finite verbs, the sequence of fragmentary sentences does create effects that Dickens could not have achieved—or achieved as well—with complete sentences.

The points to be made in citing these examples of spoken and written discourse are (1) that sentence fragments are a part of the

English language (in that sense, they are "grammatical"), (2) that in certain contexts they do communicate meaning, and (3) that, in some circumstances and for some purposes, they are appropriate and therefore acceptable, effective, and even stylistically desirable. The key to the appropriate use of a sentence fragment is being aware of what you are doing. You should be aware that you are deliberately using a sentence fragment instead of a complete sentence, and you should have some purpose or effect in mind when you use that sentence fragment. Likewise, you should always be aware of the possibility that a sentence fragment may not be acceptable to some readers and may not communicate your ideas clearly.

12 Confusing Sentences

Choose words and put them together so that they make sense.

A confusing or puzzling sentence is one that, because of some flaw in the *choice* of words or in the *arrangement* of words, reveals no meaning or a scrambled meaning or a vague meaning. This flaw of diction or arrangement produces what might be called a "non-English" sentence—a sentence that is semantically or grammatically impossible in the English language. For example, a sentence like "The ice cube froze" is a non-English sentence because of the choice of semantically incompatible words: **ice cube** and **froze.** We can say "The water froze," but we are uttering nonsense if we say "The ice cube froze." A sentence like "Harshly me teacher scolded the yesterday" is a non-English sentence because English grammar does not allow that arrangement of words. To make sense, those words would have to be arranged in an order like "The teacher scolded me harshly yesterday."

Sample revisions:

> **Original (1):** In these particular cases that I have heard about, **result in the person paying for the towing bill and the parking.**

Revision: In these particular cases that I have heard about, the result is that the offender pays the towing bill and the parking bill.

Original (2): In addition, I will utilize human factors engineering concepts to produce a **man-machine interface** that will improve the operation of the assembly line.

Revision: In addition, I will utilize human factors and engineering concepts to produce a robot that will improve the operation of the assembly line.

Original (3): The cost of insulating a house in this region is more than repaid **in rapidly advancing economy with greater material comforts homewise and for peace of mind.**

Revision: The cost of insulating a house in this region is more than repaid in rapidly accelerated savings and in the ever-increasing material comforts in the home that can produce peace of mind.

Original (4): These methods are not considered ideal for routine **tests because of however you think of them** boredom sets in and the patients lose interest in the process.

Revision: These methods are not considered ideal for routine tests because, regardless of what you think of the methods, boredom sets in and the patients lose interest in the process.

Original (5): William Faulkner presents in his short story "Barn Burning" **a character that is as nonhuman as is feasible to a person's mind.**

Revision: William Faulkner presents in his short story "Barn Burning" a character who is as unlike a human being as a person could imagine.

Explanation:

Some of the sample sentences above are confusing or puzzling mainly because of the choice of words. For instance, in sentence 2, the choice of words **man-machine interface** is puzzling, and in sentence

3, the choice of **economy** is confusing. In sentence 5, there is some incompatibility between **character** and **nonhuman,** and the word **feasible** does not fit in that context.

The other two sample sentences are examples of confusing or puzzling sentences produced by faulty syntax (arrangement of words). The writers of those sentences started out on a certain track but got derailed, or they switched to another track. Sentence 1, for instance, starts out well—**In these particular cases that I have heard about**—but then gets derailed. Sentence 4 starts out on one track and then switches to another.

If reading your sentences aloud does not help you to detect confusing or puzzling sentences, you may wish to have a peer reader point out sentences which are confusing. Using a "say-back" technique to allow a reader to paraphrase or say back to you what that reader thinks you are saying may help you to see both why the sentence is confusing and how it can be made clear.

13 Comma Splices, Fused Sentences, and Run-ons

Independent clauses cannot be spliced simply with a comma or run together without any punctuation.

Comma splices:

A comma splice is the result of joining independent clauses with nothing but a comma. *A comma is a separating device, not a joining device.* A comma splice is therefore an error in punctuation, but since punctuation is, for the written language, the grammatical equivalent of vocal intonation in the spoken language, this error in punctuation can also be considered an error in grammar.

Independent clauses must be joined either by a coordinating conjunction (**and, but, or, for, nor, yet, so**) or by a semicolon. In addition to these two ways of properly splicing independent clauses, there are two other ways of fixing a comma splice: by making separate sentences of the two clauses and by subordinating one of the clauses. The table below illustrates these four means of fixing comma splices. These four ways of repairing comma splices are equally justifiable, but one of them will usually prove to be stylistically preferable.

Ways to Repair Comma Splices

13

1. Insert the appropriate coordinating conjunction after the comma:

   We do not have to infer the author's purpose, **for** it is spelled out quite clearly for us.

2. Substitute a semicolon for the comma:

   We do not have to infer the author's purpose**;** it is spelled out quite clearly for us.

3. Put a period at the end of the first independent clause and begin a new sentence with the first word of the second independent clause:

   We do not have to infer the author's purpose. **It** is spelled out quite clearly for us.

4. Subordinate one of the independent clauses:

   We do not have to infer the author's purpose, **because** it is spelled out quite clearly for us.

   or

   Because it is spelled out clearly for us, we do not have to infer the author's purpose.

Sample revisions:

Original (1): There are very few weather features that remain the same for any length of time, it is not those same features that directly affect an area forecast.

Revision: There are very few weather features that remain the same for any length of time, **and** it is not those same features that directly affect an area forecast.

Original (2): As for the material we will use, steel is relatively inexpensive, **however** it is very heavy.

Revision: As for the material we will use, steel is relatively inexpensive, **but** it is very heavy.

Original (3): It was not worth my while to argue with her, I just ignored her and went away.

Revision: It was not worth my while to argue with her**;** I just ignored her and went away.

Original (4): My adviser was very helpful, he spent hours trying to explain to me the logic behind his recommendations.

Revision: My adviser was very helpful. **He** spent hours trying to explain to me the logic behind his recommendations.

Fused sentences or run-on sentences:

The term commonly used to label two or more independent clauses that have been run together without any conjunction or punctuation is *fused sentence* or *run-on sentence*. Fused sentences are not as common in writing as comma splices, but when they occur, they are even more of a stumbling block for readers than comma splices. Reading sentences aloud can help writers to detect natural stopping places in their writing—places where the expression of one thought ends and the expression of another begins. Fused sentences, once detected, can usually be revised in the same four ways that comma splices can be revised as illustrated in the table which follows.

Ways to Revise Fused or Run-on Sentences

1. Join the independent clauses with the appropriate coordinating conjunction.

   Original: My piano lessons were not very beneficial to me I was always too tired to practice.

   Revision: My piano lessons were not very beneficial to me, for I was always too tired to practice.

2. Splice the independent clauses with a semicolon.

   Original: There are some commuters who don't even bother to park on campus instead they park in the streets east of the university.

   Revision: There are some commuters who don't even bother to park on campus; instead, they park in the streets east of the campus.

3. Make separate sentences of the independent clauses.

   Original: Nobody in the stands could tell which horse had won the race in fact even the officials could not tell after looking at the photographs of the finish.

   Revision: Nobody in the stands could tell which horse had won the race. In fact, even the officials could not tell after looking at the photographs of the finish.

4. Subordinate one of the independent clauses.

   Original: I admit that she is honest nevertheless I will not vote for her.

   Revision: Although I admit that she is honest, I will not vote for her.

13

As with comma splices, all four of these ways of revising are usually appropriate for correcting a fused or run-on sentence. But in a particular instance, one may appear to be a better choice than another. For instance, the sentence **Why am I qualified to speak on this subject I just finished three dreadful years of high school** represents the fusion of both a question and a statement. Thus, it most readily lends itself to revision by separation of the two utterances: **Why am I qualified to speak on this subject? I just finished three dreadful years of high school.**

A sentence like **All the apples were picked before the first frost but many of them were unfit to eat** may appear to be a fused or run-on sentence, but in fact, it is not. Unlike the other examples in this section on fused sentences, this utterance has the coordinating conjunction **but** to join the two independent clauses. It lacks the comma called for in compound sentences and thus demonstrates an error in punctuation. Simply placing a comma before the coordinating conjunction **but** would correct the sentence.

14

14 Subject/Verb Agreement

The predicate verb should agree in number with its subject.

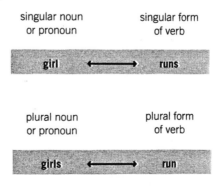

singular noun
or pronoun

singular form
of verb

girl ⟷ runs

plural noun
or pronoun

plural form
of verb

girls ⟷ run

Sample revisions:

Original (1): He **don't wear** a hat even in zero weather.

Revision: He **doesn't wear** a hat even in zero weather.

Original (2): The instructor's lack of teaching skills **hinder** the students' learning.

Revision: The instructor's lack of teaching skills **hinders** the students' learning.

14

Original (3): I hope you will find that my training and experience **fits** the opening that you advertised in the paper.

Revision: I hope you will find that my training and experience **fit** the opening that you advertised in the paper.

Original (4): The jury **has reached** their decision.

Revision: The jury **has reached** its decision.

Original (5): You can easily avoid most of the headaches that **comes** from dealing with the Division of Traffic and Parking.

Revision: You can easily avoid most of the headaches that **come** from dealing with the Division of Traffic and Parking.

Explanation:

Expressions like **He don't wear a hat even in zero weather** are not so much "mistakes" in agreement as carryovers from the dialect that people speak, quite acceptably, in their own communities. Writers should be aware of the standard form of the verb in written prose: **He doesn't wear a hat even in zero weather** (a singular verb with a singular subject).

Most errors of agreement in written prose are the result of carelessness, inadvertence, or uncertainty. The writer often knows better but merely slips up. Errors in agreement often occur when several words intervene between the simple subject of the sentence and the predicate verb, as in sentence 2: **The instructor's lack of teaching skills hinder the students' learning.** The simple subject of that sentence is **lack,** but because the plural noun **skills** (the object of the preposition **of**) intervenes between that singular subject and the verb, the writer was influenced to use the plural form of the verb (**hinder**) instead of the correct singular form (**hinders**). Careful proofreading will often catch such inadvertent errors of agreement.

14

Errors due to uncertainty are another matter. Uncertainty about whether the verb should be singular or plural arises in cases where (1) the subject is compound, (2) the subject is a collective noun, (3) the subject follows the structure **there is/there are,** and (4) the subject takes the form of a special structure, such as **one of those who** or **this person as well as.**

Creating appropriate subject/verb agreement in uncertain cases:

Compound subject:

1. Singular subjects joined by **and** usually take a plural verb.

   John and his sister **were questioned** by the police.

   I hope that you will find that my training and experience **fit** the opening that you advertised in the newspaper.

2. Singular subjects joined by **or** or by the correlative conjunctions **either . . . or** or **neither . . . nor** take a singular verb.

   John or his sister **runs** the store during the week.

   Neither the nurse nor Dr. Bruce **is worried** about the patient's condition.

3. When both subjects are plural, the verb is plural.

   The detectives and the insurance agents **have expressed** their belief in the innocence of the brother and sister.

Neither the detectives nor the insurance agents **have expressed** any doubts about the innocence of the brother and sister.

4. When one subject is singular and the other subject is plural and the subjects are joined by **or** or by the correlative conjunctions **either . . . or, neither . . . nor,** or **not only . . . but** the verb agrees in number with the closer subject.

Either John or his parents **work** in the store on Sunday.

Neither the brothers nor the sister appears to be cooperative.

Not only the brother but also the sister **appears** to be cooperative.

14

However, plural or singular subjects joined by the correlative conjunctions **both . . . and** take a plural verb.

Both John and his sister **have agreed** to cooperate with the police.

Collective noun as subject:

1. If the collective noun is viewed as a group, the verb is singular.

The jury **has made** up its mind.

The committee **was elected** unanimously.

The percentage of students who failed **has increased** by 50 percent.

2. If the collective noun is considered as *individuals*, each acting on his or her own, the verb is plural.

The jury **have made** up their minds

The committee **wish** to offer their congratulations to the new chairperson.

A number of students **have asked** the dean for an extension.

The structure *there is/there are* or *there was/there were:*

1. If the delayed or real subject following **there** is singular, the verb is singular.

There **is** a remarkable consensus among the committee members.

2. If the delayed or real subject following **there** is plural, the verb is plural.

There **were** ten dissenting votes among the stockholders.

Special structures:

14

1. In the structure **one of the [plural noun—e.g., *women*] who,** the predicate verb of the **who** clause is plural, because the antecedent of the subject **who** is the plural noun rather than the singular **one.**

Lou Holtz is one of the coaches who **refuse** to recognize the tradition. (Here the antecedent of **who** is the plural noun **coaches.**)

2. **An exception:** If **the only** precedes **one of the [plural noun—e.g., *coaches*] who,** the predicate verb of the **who** clause is singular, because the subject of **who** refers to the singular **one** rather than to the plural object of the preposition **of.**

Lou Holtz is the only one of the coaches who **refuses** to recognize the tradition.

3. A singular subject followed by structures such as **as well as, in addition to,** and **together with** takes a singular verb. (Of course, a plural subject followed by any of these structures would take a plural verb. See the third example below.)

The sergeant, as well as his superior officer, **praises** his platoon.

Steven Spielberg, along with George Lucas, **acknowledges** the potential success of this film.

These viruses, together with their complications, **prohibit** a likely recovery of the patient.

4. Nouns that do not end in -s but that are plural in meaning take a plural verb.

The bacteria **require** constant attention.

These data are consistent with the company's own findings.

The deer **do** not **represent** a major threat to plant life in this area.

5. Nouns that end in -s but are singular in meaning take a singular verb.

My grandmother's scissors **was** very dull.

Four thousand dollars **is** a fair price for a used car.

Our business took its genesis in the common complaint that two months **seems** like a long time to wait for a tax refund.

15

6. Noun clauses serving as the subject of the sentence always take a singular verb.

That he postponed the decision to merge the two divisions **has** the CEO's approval.

What created the controversy **was** a misreading of the initial documentation.

7. In inverted structures, where the subject follows the verb, a singular subject takes a singular verb, and a plural subject takes a plural verb.

How intense **were** their gazes!

Among the materials you have received **are** the tax data, all invoices, and the accounts receivable.

15 Noun/Pronoun Agreement

A pronoun must agree in person, number, and gender with its antecedent noun (the noun that precedes the pronoun).

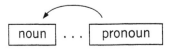

Pronouns, which are substitutes for nouns, share the following features with nouns: **number** (singular or plural) and **gender** (masculine or feminine or neuter). What nouns and pronouns do not share is the full range of person. All nouns are **third person** exclusively, but some pronouns are **first person** (**I, we**), some are **second person** (**you**), and some are **third person** (**he, she, it, they, one, some, none, all, everybody**).

15

A pronoun must correspond with whatever features of person, number, and gender it has in common with its antecedent noun.

Sample revisions:

Original (1): Even early in the morning, **no one** should expect to get a parking space close to the building where **they** work.

Revision: Even early in the morning, **no one** should expect to get a parking space close to the building where **he or she** works.

or

Even early in the morning, **people** should not expect to get parking spaces close to the buildings where **they** work.

Original (2): Each student was allowed to voice **their** opinion on the issue being discussed.

Revision: Each student was allowed to voice **his or her** opinion on the issue being discussed.

or

All students were allowed to voice **their opinions** on the issue being discussed.

Original (3): Many **words** in our language can claim television as **its** birthplace.

Revision: Many **words** in our language can claim television as **their** birthplace.

Original (4): A family cannot go camping these days without a truck-load of gadgets to make **your** campsite look like home.

Revision: A family cannot go camping these days without a truck-load of gadgets to make **its** campsite look like home.

Original (5): Every **man** has to deal with problems that did not concern **them** in civilian life.

Revision: Every **man** has to deal with problems that did not concern **him** in civilian life.

15

Explanation:

The first two sample sentences exhibit the problem writers have with noun-pronoun agreement because the English language has no convenient pronoun for indicating masculine-or-feminine gender. It has been a common practice to use the generic **he** (**him, his**) to refer to nouns of common gender like **student, teacher, writer, candidate,** or **driver.** However, in recent years, the use of the generic **he** and its derivative forms (**his, him**) to refer to singular nouns that could be either masculine or feminine has come to be considered an example of sexist bias in the English language. Most writers today avoid offending readers with any kind of sexist language. Therefore, we dealt with the problem of noun/pronoun agreement either by using the phrase **he or she** in place of the faulty plural pronoun: "Even early in the morning, no **one** should expect to get a parking space close to the building where **he or she** works," *or* by changing the subject to a plural to correspond to the plural pronoun following it. That is, instead of using **each student** as the subject of the sentence, we changed the subject to the plural form, **all students,** and then we used the plural pronoun **their** to refer to **students:** All **students** were allowed to voice **their** opinions on the issue being discussed.

Mismatchings of nouns and pronouns in person and gender are not very common in written prose. Most mismatchings of nouns and pronouns involve number—a singular pronoun referring to a plural noun (**words . . . it,** as in sentence 3 above) or a plural pronoun referring to a singular noun (**man . . . them,** as in sentence 5). Another agreement problem derives from the ambiguity of a number of such pronouns as **everyone, all, none, some,** and **each.** Although there are exceptions, the following guidelines are generally reliable.

15

Creating Appropriate Noun/Pronoun Agreement with *Everyone, All, None, Some,* and *Each*

Everyone, everybody, anybody, and *anyone* invariably take singular verbs and, in formal usage at least, should be referred to by a singular pronoun.

Examples: Everyone brings **his or her** schedule cards to the bursar's office.

Anybody who wants to run in the race has to pay her entry fee by Friday.

All and **some** are singular or plural according to the context. If the **of** phrase following the pronoun specifies a mass or bulk of something, the pronoun is singular. If the **of** phrase specifies a number of things or persons, the pronoun is plural.

Examples: Some of the fabric has lost **its** coloring.

All of the sugar was spoiled by **its** own chemical imbalance.

Some of the students complained about **their** dormitory rooms.

All of the women registered their protests at City Hall.

None is singular or plural according to the context. (The distinction in particular cases is sometimes so subtle that a writer could justify either a singular or a plural pronoun.)

Examples: None of the young men **was** willing to turn in **his** driver's license. (*But* **were . . . their** *could also be justified in this case.*)

> **None** of the young men **were** as tall as **their** fathers. (*Here it would be harder to justify the singular forms* **was . . . his.**)

Each is singular.

> **Example: Each** of the mothers declared **her** undying allegiance to democracy.

For guidelines about the number of collective nouns (like **family** and **team**), see section 14.

16

If you match up your pronouns in person, number, and gender with their antecedent nouns, you will make it easier for your reader to figure out what the pronouns refer to.

16 Pronoun/Antecedent Agreement

A pronoun should have a clear antecedent.

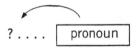

? . . . .   pronoun

Careless handling of the pronoun often blocks communication between writer and reader. As the writer, you usually know what you meant the pronoun to stand for, but if there is no antecedent (a noun in the previous group of words to which the pronoun can refer) or if it is difficult to find the noun to which the pronoun refers, your reader will not know—and will have to guess—what the pronoun stands for.

Sample revisions:

> **Original (1):** The Acme Corporation has taken the safety program too lightly. In fact, **it** has taken **it** so lightly that **it** has cost the company over $7 million in insurance claims.

Revision: The Acme Corporation has taken the safety program too lightly. In fact, **it** has taken the program so lightly that **this indifference** has cost the company over $7 million in insurance claims.

Original (2): Marilyn told her mother that **her** purse was on the dresser.

Revision: Marilyn told her mother, "Your purse is on the dresser."

or

Marilyn told her mother, "My purse is on the dresser."

Original (3): The definition of *dude* is remarkably similar to the definition of *dandy* or *fop*. **This** raises the question of whether the word *dude* really has a meaning distinctive from that of the other two words.

Revision: The definition of *dude* is remarkably similar to the definition of *dandy* or *fop*. **This similarity** raises the question of whether the word *dude* really has a meaning distinctive from that of the other two words.

Original (4): Note that this area on the monitor screen is quite near the menu of this software program, **which** is intentional.

Revision: Note that this area on the monitor screen is quite near the menu of this software program, a placement that is intentional.

or

Note that this area on the monitor screen is quite intentionally placed near the menu of this software program.

Original (5): This method sidesteps what most sophomores would do, **which** is to consult their advisers.

Revision: This method sidesteps what most sophomores would do: they would consult their advisers.

Original (6): The team's decision was to cancel all doubleheaders on the schedule, but **it** could not get the approval of the other teams in the league.

Revision: The team decided to cancel all doubleheaders on the schedule, but **it** could not get the approval of the other teams in the league.

Explanation:

16

Whenever you use a pronoun, check to see whether there is a noun in the previous group of words that could be put into the place of the pronoun. You want to avoid using the same pronoun in a sentence when each one refers to a different antecedent. In the first revised sentence above, for instance, **it** is used three times. The first time **it** refers to **Acme Corporation;** the second time **it** refers to **safety program.** To what word does the third **it** refer? We have revised the sentence to remove unclear references: **The Acme Corporation has taken the safety program too lightly. In fact, it has taken the program so lightly that this indifference has cost the company over $7 million in insurance claims.** With this revision, the reader should have no question about what the two sentences are saying.

In the second example sentence, the pronoun reference is unclear because the pronoun **her** could refer to Marilyn or to her mother. Because the context in which the sentence occurred didn't help us to determine whose purse was being referred to, we revised the sentence in two ways, turning the sentence into a direct quotation which identifies the owner of the purse clearly.

Although the use of the pronoun **this** or **that** to refer to a whole idea in a previous clause or sentence has long been a common practice in spoken English, writers need to be aware that by using the demonstrative pronoun **this** or **that** in that way, they may run the risk that the reference of the pronoun will be vague or ambiguous to readers. To avoid that risk, you can use **this** or **that** (or the corresponding plurals **these** or **those**) as an adjective instead of as a pronoun. The adjective is placed before a noun indicating what **this** or **that** stands for. In sentence 3, we eliminated the vague pronoun reference by using the phrase **this similarity** instead of the less specific pronoun **this.**

The use of the relative pronoun **which** or **that** to refer to a whole idea in the main clause rather than to a specific noun is also becoming more common. But there is a disadvantage in this use similar to the one that attends the use of **this** or **that** to refer to a whole idea. We tried to save the reader from being momentarily baffled by the **which** in sentence 4 by supplying a summary noun to serve as the antecedent for the relative pronoun. In revising sentence 4, we have inserted **placement** as the antecedent for the relative pronoun **that.** Since it is impossible to invent a noun antecedent for the **which** in sentence 5, we had to resort to another kind of revision strategy: we put a complete sentence after a colon.

The problem with the pronoun reference in sentence 6 stems from the linguistic fact that a pronoun does not readily reveal its antecedent if it refers to a noun that is located in a subordinate structure such as a possessive (the **school's** principal), a modifier of a noun (the **school** term), or an object of a preposition (in the **school**). One way to revise for pronoun reference in sentence 6 is to use the noun **team** in the second clause rather than the pronoun **it.** We thought it sounded less repetitive to revise the sentence by making **team** the subject of the first clause so that the **it** in the second clause would have a clear antecedent.

17 Verb Forms

Use the proper form of the verb.

Native speakers of English are often not aware of how subtly complicated the English verb system is, especially the system of tenses, which indicate the time of an action or a state of being. But non-native-speakers who have had to learn English in school are painfully aware of the subtleties of the English verb system. English is doubly difficult for those whose native languages do not have a system of tenses for their verbs. Instead of indicating time by making some change in the form of the verb (e.g., **walk, walked; sleep, slept**), these languages indicate time by adding some word to the sentence—as English sometimes does to indicate future time, even when the verb indicates present time (e.g., **She goes tomorrow**).

17

Native speakers of English, who learn the language in the natural way, as a part of the normal process of growing up, usually handle the complicated verb system quite well. Occasionally, however, most of us use the wrong form of a verb, as did the writers of the sample sentences which follow. Let us revise these sentences and then review some of the basic conventions governing the formation of the past tense and the past participle of the English verb.

Sample revisions:

Original (1): Before this change was made in the work schedule, some workers **use** to arrive a half hour before the plant gates were opened.

Revision: Before this change was made in the work schedule, some workers **used** to arrive a half hour before the plant gates were opened.

Original (2): Hence, much effort **has went** into the design of this traffic control system.

Revision: Hence, much effort **has gone** into the design of this traffic control system.

Original (3): Yesterday, when the foreman left his glasses **laying** on the workbench, he walked off without them.

Revision: Yesterday, when the foreman left his glasses **lying** on the workbench, he walked off without them.

Explanation:

The omission of the **-d** at the end of **use** in sentence 1 is understandable, because in speaking, we are scarcely conscious of pronouncing the final **-d**. But this expression must always be written as **used to.** In sentence 2, the writer has used the wrong form of the main verb with the auxiliary verb **has** (**has went** instead of **has gone**). In the **when** clause of sentence 3, the writer has used the incorrect transitive verb **laying** for the correct intransitive verb **lying.**

Most of the errors that writers make with verbs involve a lack of agreement in person or number between the subject and verb or the wrong past-tense form or the wrong past-participle form. Subject-predicate agreement is dealt with in section 14. The present section has dealt mainly with improper past-tense and past-participle forms. The majority of English verbs form their past tense and past participle by adding **-ed** or **-d** to the stem form (e.g., **walk, walked; believe, believed**). These verbs are called *regular verbs,* or sometimes *weak verbs.*

The so-called *irregular verbs* or *strong verbs* form their past tense and past participle by means of a change in spelling (e.g., **sing, sang, sung; hide, hid, hidden**). If you do not know, or are not sure of, the principal parts of these verbs, consult a good dictionary, which supplies the past tense and the past participle of all irregular verbs. But for your convenience, the principal parts of the most commonly used irregular verbs are presented on the following page. (Incidentally, the *stem form* of the verb is the form that combines with *to* to become the infinitive: **to walk, to go.** The stem form is also the form that the verb has when it is used with first-person pronouns in the present tense: **I walk, we go.**)

17

Principal Parts of Some Irregular Verbs

Stem form	Past-tense form	Past-participle form
begin	began	begun
bite	bit	bitten
blow	blew	blown
break	broke	broken
choose	chose	chosen
do	did	done
drink	drank	drunk
drive	drove	driven
eat	ate	eaten
fall	fell	fallen
fly	flew	flown
forget	forgot	forgotten
give	gave	given
go	went	gone
know	knew	known
lay	laid	laid
lie	lay	lain
pay	paid	paid
ride	rode	ridden
ring	rang	rung
rise	rose	risen
run	ran	run
see	saw	seen
sit	sat	sat
speak	spoke	spoken
swear	swore	sworn
take	took	taken
throw	threw	thrown
wear	wore	worn

17

18 Placement of Modifiers

Misplaced modifiers lead to a misreading of the sentence.

Misplaced modifiers:

18

Because English is a language that depends heavily on word order to protect meaning, related words, phrases, and clauses should be placed as close as possible to one another. Adverbial and adjectival modifiers especially must be placed as close as possible to words that they modify. Failure to juxtapose related words, phrases, or clauses may lead to a misreading, that is, to a reading different from what the author intended.

Sample revisions:

Original (1): The plan that they formulated **quickly** forced them to assume a strong position.

Revision: The plan that they **quickly** formulated forced them to assume a strong position.

or

The plan that they formulated forced them **quickly** to assume a strong position.

Original (2): In the School of Architecture, students are **only** permitted to enter the program in the fall of the year.

Revision: In the School of Architecture, students are permitted to enter the program **only** in the fall of the year.

Original (3): I had already thought about how the roller could be adapted **at the outset of the project.**

Revision: At the outset of the project, I had already thought about how the roller could be adapted.

Original (4): Emil **even** limps when nobody is watching him.

Revision: Emil limps **even** when nobody is watching him.

Original (5): She paid $180 for a dress at the local boutique **that she despised.**

Revision: At the local boutique, she paid $180 for a dress **that she despised.**

Original (6): The teacher handed out application forms to her students **stained with splotches of ink.**

18

Revision: The teacher handed out to her students application forms **stained with splotches of ink.**

Explanation:

In sentence 1, we have an example of what is called a "squinting modifier," a modifier that looks in two directions at once. In that sentence, the adverb **quickly** sits between two verbs that it could modify: **formulated** and **forced.** If the writer intends that adverb to modify the act of *formulating* rather than the act of *forcing,* the position of **quickly** should be shifted so that the sentence reads as follows: **The plan that they quickly formulated forced them to assume a strong position.** If, however, the writer intends the adverb to modify the act of *forcing,* **quickly** should be shifted to a position between **them** and **to assume.**

Because the adverb **only** in sentence 2 is placed before the verb **permitted,** it is modifying a word that the author did not intend it to modify. **Only** should be shifted to a position before the phrase that the author meant it to modify: **only in the fall of the year.**

Because the prepositional phrase **at the outset of the project** has been put in the wrong place in sentence 3, it does not modify the verb phrase that it should be modifying (**had thought**) and therefore does not say what the writer intended to say. Note that in the revision of sentence 3, the prepositional phrase has been shifted to the beginning of the sentence so that it will modify what it should be modifying.

Chances are that the writer of sentence 4 did not intend **even** to modify the act of *limping*. Shifting **even** will make the sentence say what the writer probably meant to say: **Emil limps even when nobody is watching him.**

In sentences 5 and 6, shifting the modifier closer to the noun that it modifies makes the sentences say what the writers meant to say.

18

Dangling modifiers:

Another way that writers "misplace" modifiers is to allow the modifiers to dangle. In English, an introductory verbal phrase naturally modifies the subject of the main clause. When the subject of the main clause is *not* the "doer" of the action indicated in the verbal, we say that the verbal dangles.

Sample revisions:

Original (1): Revolving at a rate of 2,200 revolutions per minute, the janitor turned off the overheated generator.

Revision: Revolving at a rate of 2,200 revolutions per minute, the overheated generator was turned off by the janitor.

or

The janitor turned off the overheated generator, which was revolving at a rate of 2,200 revolutions per minute.

Original (2): After finding a good adviser, your next challenge will be to make an appointment with that person at a convenient time.

Revision: After finding a good adviser, you should make an appointment with that person at a convenient time.

Original (3): To facilitate this operation, measurements will be taken of the distance that the throw-arm travels whenever a box is discharged from the assembly line.

Revision: To facilitate this operation, the engineers will measure the distance that the throw-arm travels whenever a box is discharged from the assembly line.

Original (4): In order to study the effects of sudden surges, it is necessary to monitor a series of voltage variations.

Revision: In order to study the effects of sudden surges, the attendant must monitor a series of voltage variations.

19

Explanation:

Sometimes in revising the sentence to make the subject of the main clause the doer of the action specified in our introductory verbal, we have to resort to a rather awkward passive verb, as we did in sentence 1. If we start a sentence with a verbal phrase, we cannot start the main clause of the sentence with a structure like **there is** or **it is** (see sentence 4). To prevent dangling verbals, writers should always make sure that the subject of the main clause is the doer of the action specified in the preceding verbal. Reading sentences aloud will sometimes indicate the misplacement of modifying words, phrases, and clauses.

19 Subordinate Conjunction *that*

Use the subordinate conjunction *that* if it will prevent a possible misreading.

Because we like to economize on our language, we often omit syllables in contractions such as **he's, she'll, we'd,** and **won't,** and we resort to such common elliptical expressions as **not all [of] the men,** she is taller than I [am tall], and when [I was] in the fourth grade. We also frequently omit the conjunction that, which introduces a noun clause serving as the object of a verb, as in "He said [that] he was going" and "He announced [that] I was a candidate for office."

Deciding whether to use the conjunction that in written prose will be a problem only when a noun clause is being used as the direct object of a verb—but not in every instance of such use. If there is no chance that a sentence will be misread, it is all right, even in written prose, to omit that. But if there is a chance that the noun phrase following the verb may be read as the object of the verb rather than as the subject of the subsequent clause, we can prevent even a momentary misreading by inserting that at the beginning of the noun clause.

19

Sample revisions:

Original (1): Dr. Meyers will discover   the space where he parked his car is empty.

Revision: Dr. Meyers will discover **that** the space where he parked his car is empty.

Original (2): My father believed   his doctor, who was a boyhood friend, was wholly trustworthy.

Revision: My father believed **that** his doctor, who was a boyhood friend, was wholly trustworthy.

Original (3): Keep in mind   this university has many opportunities to offer.

Revision: Keep in mind **that** this university has many opportunities to offer.

Original (4): Students need to make sure not only that they promptly apply for financial aid but   the aid arrives in time for them to pay their fees.

Revision: Students need to make sure not only that they promptly apply for financial aid but **that** the aid arrives in time for them to pay their fees.

Original (5): The police reported ⊛ as soon as they found out that the car was stolen, they sent out a description of it to all the squad cars on duty.

Revision: The police reported **that** as soon as they found out that the car was stolen, they sent out a description of it to all the squad cars on duty.

20

Explanation:

In a sentence like "He believed they were going," it is safe to omit **that** after **believed** because **they** cannot possibly be read as the object of **believed.** (If **they** were the object of the verb here, the pronoun would have to be **them: He believed them.**) But in a sentence like 2, it is not only possible but likely that the noun phrase **his doctor** will initially be read as the object of **believed** (**he believed his doctor**). Of course, as soon as we come to the predicate **was wholly trustworthy,** we realize that we have misread the sentence as the writer intended it to be read. But the writer could have prevented that initial misreading by inserting **that** after **believed: My father believed that his doctor, who was a boyhood friend, was wholly trustworthy.** Then the sentence can be read in only one way.

20 Relative Pronouns *that, which,* and *who*

One commonly misunderstood function of the relative pronouns **that, which,** and **who** is to introduce restrictive (**that** or **who**) or nonrestrictive (**which** or **who**) adjective clauses. A restrictive adjective clause is one that identifies or specifies the particular person, place, or thing being talked about. It "restricts" the noun it modifies because it "defines" the noun it modifies. Nonrestrictive clauses give additional information about the nouns they modify, but they do not serve to identify or specify the nouns that they modify.

20 Using Relative Pronouns Appropriately in Restrictive and Nonrestrictive Clauses

Restrictive clauses modifying nonhuman nouns should be introduced with the relative pronoun **that:**

The bacterium that causes lockjaw is called *Clostridium tetani.*

Nonrestrictive clauses modifying nonhuman nouns should be introduced with the relative pronoun **which:**

The bacterium *Clostridium tetani,* which causes lockjaw, can bring death within a week of its introduction into the bloodstream.

Both restrictive and nonrestrictive clauses modifying human nouns should be introduced with *who:*

People who refuse to get tetanus shots when they incur puncture wounds risk their lives for stubbornness.

Sample revisions:

Original (1): Bottled water that is a very expensive commodity in this desert region was sold at every hundred-mile checkpoint.

Revision: Bottled water, which is a very expensive commodity in this desert region, was sold at every hundred-mile checkpoint.

Original (2): The kind of petting pool which is usually found at the entrance to such a park was located in the center of the Sea Treasures grounds.

Revision: The kind of petting pool that is usually found at the entrance to such a park was located in the center of the Sea Treasures grounds.

Original (3): The terrain that was formed by rock formations eroded by years of wind and blowing sand consists largely of mesas and buttes.

Revision: The terrain, which was formed by rock formations eroded by hundreds of years of wind and blowing sand, consists largely of mesas and buttes.

20

Explanation:

Sometimes the relative pronoun may be omitted in restrictive clauses, but it may never be omitted in nonrestrictive clauses.

In restrictive adjective clauses where the relative pronoun serves as the object of the verb of the adjective clause, the relative pronoun may be omitted. The relative pronoun in restrictive clauses may also be omitted if it serves as the object of a preposition in the adjective clause: "The chemist I gave the formula to disappeared" (here the understood *whom* or *that* serves as the object of the preposition **to**).

Optional Use of the Relative Pronoun in Restrictive Clauses	
With the relative pronoun:	The one **whom** I respect a great deal hardly notices me.
Without the relative pronoun:	The one I respect a great deal hardly notices me.

CAUTION: The relative pronoun may not be omitted when it serves as the subject of the restrictive adjective clause.

Necessary Use of the Relative Pronoun in Restrictive Clauses

Necessary relative pronoun:	He **who** exalts himself shall be humbled.
Necessary relative pronoun:	The money **that** was set aside for scholarships was squandered on roads.

20

In nonrestrictive adjective clauses, it is *not* possible to drop the relative pronoun.

Example: Joe, **whom** I respect a great deal, hardly speaks to me.
Kwong Bruce, **who** is our best engineer, will not cooperate with me.

However, it is possible in some instances to replace the nonrestrictive adjective clause with a shorter appositive phrase:

Kwong Bruce, **our best engineer,** will not cooperate with me.

It is important to learn to identify restrictive and nonrestrictive clauses because the meaning of a sentence can be changed radically if commas are not placed where they should be or are placed where they do not belong. To learn how to appropriately punctuate restrictive and nonrestrictive clauses containing the relative pronouns **that, which,** and **who,** consult sections 39 and 40.

Stylistic Choices: Sentences and Words

Style is the result of strategies that we develop for using words or sentences in a particular way. Some linguistic choices we may not, or should not, make. We may not choose what the grammar of the English language does not allow. We should not choose resources of language that we do not command. We would also be ill advised to choose words and structures that are inappropriate to the subject matter, the occasion, or the audience for our writing.

Aside from these general constraints, however, we have hundreds of decisions to make about vocabulary or syntax whenever we sit down to write. Will we use an active or a passive verb? Should we use one long sentence or several shorter ones? Does it seem more appropriate to use a formal word, an informal word, a specific word, a general word, a technical term, or an ordinary word? Which type and what placement of modifiers best suit our purposes for writing? How can we vary the length, rhythm, and structure of our sentences so that we don't deaden the attention of our readers with monotony?

On the surface, it may appear that one stylistic choice is as good as another, but if we took the time to study people's responses to our writing carefully—noticing where and asking them why they were put off or drawn in, why they were confused or enthused about not only *what* we said but *how* we said it—we would begin to see how our specific stylistic choices influenced the readers' willingness to read our work or their openness to our ideas. It is helpful, then, to think of revisions in style as strategy building. Rules of grammar determine whether a particular stylistic choice is *correct;* that is, whether a particular word, sentence, or passage of text complies with the conventions of the language. Principles of rhetoric determine whether a particular stylistic choice is *effective;* that is, whether our words, sentences, and passages of writing convey our intended meaning in a way that others view as compelling to read and appropriate to the subject matter, occasion, audience, and desired effect. The previous section dealt with what the grammar of the English language permits—or, more accurately, with what the conventions of Edited American English permits. This section on style will guide writers in making judicious choices from among the available options. Questions about style are not so much questions about *right* or *wrong* as questions about *good, better,* and *best.*

21

21 Concise Sentences (Wordy Sentences)

Cut out unnecessary words.

A "wordy" sentence is one in which a writer has used more words than are needed to say what has to be said. Inexperienced writers often believe that by using more words, they can make their writing appear more sophisticated or professional. Actually, unnecessary words only clutter up sentences and frustrate readers as they try to move through a text. The strategies that follow can help you to eliminate unnecessary words in your writing.

Ways to Eliminate Unnecessary Words

1. Highlight words that present the main idea, and construct the sentence around them.

    Original: For the average reader one would not find interest in a book of this type due to the fact that it deals mainly with martial arts. **(26 words)**

Revision: Because it deals mainly with martial arts, this book may not be of interest to many readers. **(17 words)**

or

Many readers may not like this book because it is about martial arts. **(13 words)**

2. Drop any words that don't add meaning.

21

Original: The most serious problem that is most difficult to solve in this company is the cost of the health insurance program. **(21 words)**

Revision: Health insurance costs are the most serious and difficult problem our company has to solve. **(15 words)**

or

Health insurance costs are our company's most serious and difficult problem to solve. **(13 words).**

3. Drop any writing that unnecessarily talks about writing.

Original: Of course, at this point, I have to take a minute to explain the difference between sex and gender: *sex* refers to biological makeup; *gender* reflects society's ideals of masculinity and femininity. **(32 words)**

Revision: Sex and gender differ in that a person's sex is determined by biological makeup; gender reflects society's ideals of masculinity and femininity. **(22 words)**

4. Make verbs active.

Original: Hockey and lacrosse are being looked at as possible candidates for elimination from the university. **(15 words)**

Revision: The university is considering eliminating lacrosse and hockey. **(8 words)**

21

5. Reduce phrases to words whenever possible.

> **Original:** Due to the fact that the administration has proposed major funding cuts in health programs that will reduce benefits to low-income patients by 25%, the government has increased pressure on the ADA to raise money for needy patients or provide free care for needy patients. **(46 words)**

> **Revision:** Because major funding cuts in health programs will reduce benefits to low-income patients by 25%, the government increasingly pressures the ADA to raise money or to provide free care for needy patients. **(33 words)**

6. Avoid unnecessary **There is** or **There are** constructions.

> **Original:** There was a general population growth from 1,611 to 2,301 among inmates in 1996. **(14 words)**

> **Revision:** Inmate population grew from 1,611 to 2,301 in 1996. **(9 words)**

Sample revisions:

> **Original (1):** It is my overall intent to develop a safety program into a form that is superior to the old safety format. **(21 words)**

> **Revision:** I intend to develop a safety program that is superior to the present one. **(14 words)**

> **Original (2):** The meaning, at least in my own eyes, that he is trying to convey in the poem "Arms and the Boy" is of the evilness of war in that it forces innocent people to take up instruments of death and destruction and then tries to teach them to love to use them. **(52 words)**

Revision: As I see it, the poet's thesis in "Arms and the Boy" is that war is evil, because it not only forces people to take up arms but makes them love to use these weapons to kill other human beings. **(40 words)**

Original (3): In this modern world of today, we must get an education that will prepare us for a job in our vocation in life. **(23 words)**

Revision: In the modern world, we must get an education that will prepare us for a job. **(16 words)**

21

Original (4): The prescribed weight will provide limitations for the design and use of the ladder, which when considered with the slenderness ratio will determine the ultimate design of the ladder and its components. **(32 words)**

Revision: The prescribed weight and the slenderness ratio will determine the ultimate design of the ladder and its components. **(18 words)**

Original (5): The entire assembly must be able to be carried into a cave in compact packages that should weigh less than twenty pounds. **(22 words)**

Revision: In order to be portable, the entire assembly should weigh no more than twenty pounds. **(15 words)**

Explanation:

We revised each of these sentences using the techniques described in the table above, saving from seven to fourteen words. You need not be obsessed with saving words—especially in the first draft of your writing. However, trimming back the deadwood in your final copy can help your readers. As Alexander Pope said,

> Words are like leaves, and where they most abound
> Much fruit of sense beneath is rarely found.

22 Awkward Sentences

Rephrase awkwardly constructed sentences to make them clear.

People naturally tire and turn away from any task that seems overly complex and taxing. Thus, just as readers may become frustrated by writing that asks them to wade through wordiness, so, too, they are put off by writing that is unclear.

22

In section 12, we described confusing sentences, sentences that were so unclearly structured that they revealed no meaning or only vague meaning. In this section, we deal with awkward sentences, sentences that are possible to understand but still prove very difficult for readers to tackle. Awkward sentences differ from confusing sentences in that they are grammatically passable but stylistically weak. Typically, this weakness comes from one of the sources cited in the table below.

Possible Causes of Awkward Sentences

1. Too many words, or problems with idioms:

    Original: You could get a dose of the best exercise a person could undertake, **walking.** I believe that a person should walk at a leisurely pace, **with no goal or set distance.**

    Revision: The best exercise for people is walking at a leisurely pace as far as they feel like going.

2. Words or phrases written out of their natural order:

    Original: Richard Rodriguez, though he was a child of Mexican immigrants, was continually bombarded by the English language at home **as well as Americanization through society.**

    Revision: Though he was a child of Mexican immigrants, Richard Rodriguez was immersed in speaking the English language at home and Americanized through social contacts outside the home.

3. A confusing succession of similar phrases or word forms:

Original: He was proud **of** being the president **of** the largest chapter **of** the national Fraternity **of** Students **of** Mechanical Engineering.

Revision: He was proud to serve as president in the National Fraternity of Students of Mechanical Engineering's largest chapter.

22

4. Split constructions:

Original: I, **chastened by my past experiences,** resolved never to **consciously and maliciously** circulate, **even if true,** damaging reports about my friends.

Revision: Chastened by my past experiences, I resolved never to circulate consciously and maliciously any damaging reports about my friends, even if such reports were true.

Sample revisions:

Original (1): Hiring people with the proper education **for advising** is the key **to stopping misinforming communications.**

Revision: Hiring people with the kind of education that fits them to be an adviser is the key to preventing bad communications.

Original (2): Uncertainty handling is a major concern of any diagnostic system that physicians use.

Revision: A major concern of any diagnostic system that physicians use should be its capacity to handle uncertainty.

Original (3): Parking anywhere at night is risky, **but in the campus area on side streets is probably one of the most dangerous places in the city.**

Revision: Parking anywhere at night is risky, but side streets in the campus area are probably among the most dangerous places in the city.

22

Original (4): The results of the survey were **although based on a small sampling** supportive of the benefits of TQM in most corporate situations.

Revision: Although based on a small sampling, the results of the survey support the benefits of TQM in most corporations.

Original (5): To **obtain** this level of performance, we have all taken **several required courses in design as well as have studied several elective courses in design.**

Revision: To attain this level of performance, we have all taken several required and elective courses in design.

Explanation:

Usually, writers are not aware that their sentences are awkward or clumsy because they know what is intended in the sentence and can often "read beyond" their own words to make meaning. Readers, however, do not have the same prior knowledge as the writer. Therefore, they are more likely to stumble in making meaning from odd-sounding combinations of words. To help identify sentence problems that might cause difficulties for readers, try reading backward through the text, sentence by sentence. In this way, you can focus on what is said and how it is said in a particular sentence rather than skim over the sentence because you know the gist of the text as a whole.

23 Varying Sentences

Vary sentences in length and structure to make writing not only clear but interesting.

Sentence length:

Once you have completed the first full draft of your ideas, read through the text aloud, listening to the rhythm of your reading. If the cadence seems monotonous because too many sentences are long and involved or choppy because too many sentences are very short, look for opportunities to change sentence length. Short sentences (like sentence 2 below) create emphasis as well as variety in paragraphs with many long, complicated structures.

23

Example of Varied Sentence Length

Lawyers should also be ethically responsible, taking only the cases they believe in if they have a choice. *Most lawyers have a choice.* To take on a rich client who can finance stacking the jury or offer a big payoff if you win despite his guilt is not ethical. While even this type of client has the right to representation, a lawyer is sacrificing justice for personal gain in deciding to create a defense for someone whose innocence is highly doubtful or indefensible. **(short sentence used for emphasis and variation)**

Sentence structure:

Writing also seems monotonous when all of the sentences follow the same basic sentence pattern. To vary sentence structure, try the following strategies.

Ways to Vary Sentence Structure

1. Alter sentence beginnings:

   Original: Advertisers must be persuasive to do this, and their audience expects them also to be entertaining.

   Alteration: To do this, advertisers must be persuasive and entertaining.

2. Rearrange word order:

   Original (1): All other weaknesses stemmed from this basic one.

   Rearrangement: From this basic weakness stemmed all others.

   Original (2): The Republicans are in favor of less government intervention, of course.

   Rearrangement: The Republicans, of course, are in favor of less government intervention.

   or

   Of course, the Republicans are in favor of less government intervention.

3. Use subordination: (For further explanation of subordination, see section 24; for punctuation of subordination, see section 36.)

   Original: More people are pushed into the labor force, and then the participation in the union increases.

   Subordination: As more people are pushed into the labor force, participation in the union increases.

23

The sentences in the table above show you how to make a given type of alteration in sentence structure. In the revisions that follow, we have placed those same isolated sentences in context. In each case, the choices made in revising the sentences were not the only ones possible. Each choice was made as part of a strategy for getting the ideas across in a clear and engaging way.

Sample revisions:

23

Original (1): Right-to-work laws were established to give those people who want to work the incentive and opportunity to do so. They tend to increase union membership. More people are supposedly pushed into the labor force, and then the participation in the union increases.

Revision: Right-to-work laws were established to give those people who want to work the incentive and opportunity to do so. When more people are brought into the workforce, participation in the union increases. Thus, we can say these laws increase union membership.

Original (2): Advertisers are, of course, concerned with selling their product. They must be persuasive to do this, and the audience expects them also to be entertaining. They may not lie about their products, though. Advertisers are obliged not to say Tide will get out a bloodstain if, in fact, it won't.

Revision: Advertisers, of course, are concerned with selling their product. To do this, advertisers must be both persuasive and entertaining. Advertisers may not lie about their products, though. If Tide won't get out a bloodstain, the advertisers are obliged not to say it will.

Original (3): The basic weakness of the Articles of Confederation was that the document allowed the thirteen colonies to retain too much sovereignty and independence. The Articles didn't grant the

Continental Congress enough power to conduct national and international affairs. All other weaknesses stemmed from this basic one.

Revision: The basic weakness of the Articles of Confederation was that the document allowed the thirteen colonies to retain too much sovereignty and independence. As a result, the Articles didn't grant the Continental Congress enough power to conduct national and international affairs. From this basic weakness stemmed all others.

24

24 Coordination and Subordination

Use coordination when elements in a sentence are equally important in meaning.

Use subordination when one element of a sentence is less important than others.

To prevent choppiness in your writing or to be clearer in describing close relationships among ideas, you may decide to combine several sentences into one compound (coordinating) sentence or one complex (subordinating) sentence. While there are no rules to help you decide *which* to use (the choice is made based on the type of relationships the writer wants to show between ideas), there are rules about *how* to construct these two types of sentences correctly. When writers are careless or are unclear about how to construct compound or complex sentences, they often end up creating sentence fragments, fused or run-on sentences, awkward sentences, or poorly punctuated sentences. In this section, we describe how to use coordination and subordination to combine ideas appropriately. For rules about how to punctuate these types of sentences correctly, consult section 35 and section 36.

Ways to Coordinate Ideas in Sentences

1. Use words like *and, moreover, not only . . . but also,* and *so* to join clauses (complete ideas including a subject and predicate) of like kind.

> **Original:** Thomas Jefferson liked to play the violin. Talented slaves were called upon to accompany his performances.
>
> **Coordination using *and:*** Thomas Jefferson liked to play the violin, and he called upon talented slaves to accompany him when he was performing.
>
> **Original:** The growing popularity of music in the classical period spawned new instruments like the piano. Also, a musical instrument of one kind or other was in every home.
>
> **Coordination using *moreover:*** The growing popularity of music during the classical period spawned the invention of new instruments like the piano; moreover, it introduced a musical instrument of one kind or another into almost every home.
>
> **Original:** *Full moon* refers to a lunar phase during which we can view the entire surface of the moon reflecting the sun's light and also when the moon has reached its halfway point around the earth.
>
> **Coordination using *not only . . . but also:*** Not only does the term *full moon* refer only to the lunar phase during which we can view the entire surface of the moon reflecting the sun's energy, but it also describes the phase when the moon has reached its halfway point in its revolution around the earth.

24

Original: Mozart worked and reworked entire pieces of music in his mind. Seldom did his manuscripts show revision on paper.

Coordination using *so*: Mozart worked and reworked entire pieces of music in his mind, so he seldom needed to revise his work on paper.

24

2. Use words or devices like *but, yet, however, nevertheless,* and a *semicolon* to contrast ideas in independent clauses.

Original: I liked living at home. I just didn't like to live by the rules.

Contrasting coordination using *yet*: I liked living at home, yet I didn't like having to live by the rules.

Original: Sarah has come to visit a few times, I don't see her as much as I would like to, though.

Contrasting coordination using *however*: Sarah has come to visit a few times; however, I don't see her as much as I would like to.

Original: We worked through the night to drain our basement and the water rose and eventually all our possessions were lost to the flood.

Contrasting coordination using *nevertheless*: We worked through the night to drain our basement; nevertheless, the water rose. Eventually all our possessions were lost to the flood.

Original: I was afraid I would be swept away by the strong current of the water. I got lucky, though.

Contrasting coordination using *but*: I was afraid I would be swept away by the strong current of the water, but I got lucky.

Original: Classical music was objective, orderly and had perfect form and balance, and romantic style concerned more the expression of one's feelings.

Coordination using a semicolon: Classical music was objective, orderly, and perfect in form and balance; romantic music was emotional and expressive.

24

While coordination is helpful in grouping related ideas in meaningful and stylistically effective ways, it is possible to overuse coordination so that our writing still sounds something like a grocery list of ideas. For instance, in the sentence **We worked through the night to drain our basement and the water rose and eventually all our possessions were lost to the flood,** the succession of **and**'s seems as listy as the succession of short sentences: **We worked through the night. We drained our basement. The water rose. Our possessions were lost to the flood.** One idea is simply added to another. A writer needs to look more carefully at how the main ideas of the sentences are related. Consider whether the ideas might be coordinated in a more descriptive way (as they were through coordinating contrast using **nevertheless** above) or whether some ideas might be emphasized more than others through the use of introductory phrases or through the subordination of some of the main clauses. Here are two alternative ways to revise the sentence above about the basement flood.

Revision using introductory phrases or words:

Working throughout the night, we tried to drain our basement. Sadly, though, our possessions were lost to the steady rise of the water.

Revision using subordinate clause:

Although we worked through the night to drain our basement, the water continued to rise, consuming our possessions.

Subordinate clauses can make writing very stylistically effective and prove very helpful in clarifying meaning. However, they require special handling because they contain supporting details whose meaning is not fully realized without the help of another clause in the sentence. For example:

> **Although few ancient musical instruments still exist,** descriptions of them have survived in ancient wall paintings.

24

In this sentence, the word **although** signals the reader that even though few ancient musical instruments survive, something did happen. What was it? Without knowing what did happen, we don't know how to finish the thought the writer began with the **although** clause. Therefore, we say that the **although** clause *depends* on another clause. We need both partners in this writer's thought to make the sentence complete and, thus, grammatically acceptable.

Words That Alert Readers to Subordinate Clauses

after	despite	so that	while
although	even though	that	who
as	if	unless	whoever
because	if only	until	whom
before	since	where	whose

Because subordinate clauses are used to clarify relationships for a reader, it is important to use a subordinating word that says precisely what you want it to say in precisely the right place in the sentence. Notice how the following examples of subordination, which are misleading because the writer has chosen the wrong introductory word or because the significance of the relationship between two clauses is not apparent, are revised for accuracy and clarity.

Sample revisions:

Original (1): The three outstanding composers of the classical period were Beethoven, Mozart, and Haydn. **Since these famous composers lived,** the importance of their music in the church declined. (*Since* can be misread as *because*—a misleading signal about why the music declined.)

Revision: The three outstanding composers of the classical period were Beethoven, Mozart, and Haydn. After these famous composers died, however, the importance of their music in the church declined.

24

Original (2): Although the sun is bright, the moon is luminescent. Skywatchers pay as much attention to the moon as they do the sun. (What is the significance of this comparison? In what way does one part of the sentence logically depend on the other?)

Revision: Although the moon is not as bright as the sun, its luminescence attracts as much attention from skywatchers as does the sun's brilliance.

When writers use both coordination and subordination appropriately, deliberately, and correctly, they can help readers understand quite clearly how ideas are related and can make reading lively and engaging, as in the revised passage below.

Revisions using coordination and subordination to break up monotonous sentence clusters:

Original: During one important time period of the Egyptians, four dynasties of pharaohs governed Egypt from a royal capital in Memphis. This period was called the Old Kingdom. Egypt was controlled by a central government at that time. Egyptian resources were well organized. Some of the pharaohs, like Cheops and Chephren, developed bad reputations for ruling as cruel despots. But then, at the same time, the pharaohs also built the pyramids of Giza. This gave the time a mark of distinction.

Revision: During the Egyptian time period that was called the Old Kingdom, four dynasties of pharaohs governed Egypt from a royal capital in Memphis. (subordination using a *that* clause) During that time period, Egypt was controlled by a central government, and its resources were well organized. (coordination of similarity using *and*) Some of the pharaohs, like Cheops and Chephren, developed bad reputations for ruling like cruel despots; nevertheless, they built the pyramids of Giza, which gave the time a mark of distinction. (coordination of contrast using *nevertheless;* subordination using a *which* clause)

25

25 Parallel Construction

Preserve parallel structure by using units of the same grammatical kind.

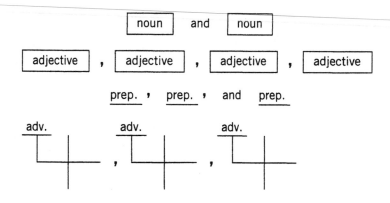

The principle governing parallel structure is that a pair or a series (three or more) of units serving the same function in a sentence should be composed of similar elements; e.g., nouns with nouns, adjectives with adjectives, not a mixture of nouns and adjectives. A breakdown in parallelism interferes with coherence because it disrupts the expectation that when a series starts out with one kind of element, it will stay with that element.

Sample revisions:

Original (1): I am now disposed **to redesign** the operation of your department or **to changing** the position of the equipment and the offices.   (infinitive phrase, gerund phrase)

25

Revision: I am now disposed **to redesign** the operation of your department or **to change** the position of the equipment and the offices.

Original (2): I also wished to find out how far a writer could go to get the precise word for the context, even if the word was not **traditional usage or grammatically correct.**   (noun, adjective)

Revision: I also wished to find out how far a writer could go to get the precise word for the context, even if the word did not conform **to traditional usage or to correct grammar.**

Original (3): The soil from the first site was **sand, infertile,** and **had a rapid percolation rate.**   (noun, adjective, and verb phrase)

Revision: The soil from the first site was **sandy, infertile,** and **rapid in percolation.**

Original (4): According to Senge, strengthening team learning involves **paying attention to your intentions, balance of advocacy with inquiry, building shared meaning, and use of self-awareness as a resource.**   (gerund, noun, gerund, noun)

Revision: According to Senge, strengthening team learning involves **paying attention to your intentions, balancing advocacy with inquiry, building shared meaning, and using self-awareness as a resource.**

Original (5): Your company and **what its potential is** are of great interest to me.   (noun, noun clause)

Revision: Your company and **its potential** are of great interest to me.

Original (6): Most programmers are forced **to either abandon** an approach to a specific problem or **to spend** hours searching for an alternative solution.   (violation of parallelism with correlative conjunctions)

25

Revision: Most programmers are forced **either to abandon** an approach to a specific problem or **to spend** hours searching for an alternative solution.

Original (7): They **not only** persuade the family that they must plan a sensible budget **but also** that a sensible budget will enable them to buy more necessities of life.   (violation of parallelism with correlative conjunctions)

Revision: They persuade the family **not only** that they must plan a sensible budget **but also** that a sensible budget will enable them to buy more of the necessities of life.

Explanation:

The obvious way to correct a breakdown in parallelism is to convert all the members of the pair or the series to units of the same structure or part of speech. In making this correction, we sometimes have an either/or option available, but usually one of the options will be stylistically preferable to the other. In revising sentence 1, for instance, we could choose the option of using a pair of gerunds instead of a pair of infinitives. If we did, the revision would take this form:

I am now disposed to redesigning the operation of your department or to changing the position of the equipment of the offices.

The other sample sentences, however, do not lend themselves as readily to alternative revisions. Sentences 6 and 7 illustrate a violation of parallelism when correlative conjunctions are used: **either . . . or, neither . . . nor, both . . . and, not only . . . but also.** The principle operating with correlative conjunctions is that the same grammatical structure must be on the right-hand side of both conjunctions. We can more easily see the breakdown in parallelism if we lay out sentence 7 in two layers:

25

They **not only** persuade the family that they must plan a sensible budget

but also that a sensible budget will enable them to buy more of the necessities of life.

On the right-hand side of **not only,** there is this grammatical sequence: a verb (**persuade**), a noun (**the family**), and a noun clause (**that a sensible budget**). But on the right-hand side of **but also,** there is only a noun clause (**that a sensible budget will enable them to buy more of the necessities of life**). The faulty parallelism can be revised in either of two ways:

They **not only** persuade the family that they must plan a sensible budget **but also** persuade the family that a sensible budget will enable them to buy more of the necessities of life.

or

They persuade the family **not only** that they must plan a sensible budget **but also** that a sensible budget will enable them to buy more of the necessities of life.

In both revisions, we now have the same grammatical structure on the right-hand side of both correlative conjunctions. But because the second revision has fewer words and less repetition than the first one, it is probably the better of the two revisions stylistically. The principle governing parallelism: **Like must be joined with like.**

26 Repetition

Avoid careless or needless repetition of words and ideas.

A careless or needless repetition is either the recurrence of a word in the same sentence or in adjoining sentences or the use of synonymous words that produce what is called a **redundancy** or **tautology.**

26

We want to be careful about cautioning writers to eliminate repetition, however, because there are instances where repetition serves a purpose. The repetition of key words can be an effective means of achieving coherence in a paragraph. And sometimes, it is better to repeat a word, even in the same sentence, than to run the risk of ambiguity or misunderstanding. In the first sentence of this paragraph, for example, the word **repetition** has been repeated because the use of the pronoun *it* in the place of **repetition** would be ambiguous. (We might wonder whether that pronoun *it* referred to **caution** or to **repetition.**) The key words to keep in mind as you assess whether repetition is appropriate, then, are **careless** and **needless.** Trim what is unnecessary and unintended.

Sample revisions:

Original (1): Jerking the heel backward suddenly and forcefully will bring the skater to a **complete stop** and increase the chance of injury.

Revision: Jerking the heel backward suddenly and forcefully will stop the skater abruptly and increase the chance of injury.

Original (2): As to the type of equipment **requirement needed,** the engineers recommend that a bonding machine be used for the laminations.

Revision: As to the type of equipment needed, the engineers recommend that a bonding machine be used for the laminations.

Original (3): I have faced this problem about the fatigue factor for some time now, and I have **thought** about it regularly **in my own mind.**

Revision: I have faced this problem about the fatigue factor for some time now, and I have thought about it regularly.

Original (4): As an introduction to opening a discussion on race, gender, and politics, it seems appropriate to quote the esteemed African-American politician Barbara Jordan.

Revision: As an introduction to a discussion on race, gender, and politics, we quote the esteemed African-American politician Barbara Jordan.

26

Original (5): The company intends to develop a **more superior** retirement program.

Revision: The company intends to develop a superior retirement program.

Original (6): It is **now inevitable** that the Internet will **eventually** become part of every household in America.

Revision: The Internet will inevitably become part of every household in America.

Original (7): The hardness of the metal increased to a certain point and **then** decreased **afterward.**

Revision: The hardness of the metal increased to a certain point and then decreased.

Explanation:

The **boldface** words in sentences 1, 2, 4, 5, 6, and 7 are instances of redundancy or tautology (needless repetition of the same idea in different words). In sentence 3, the phrase **in my own mind** is superfluous (where else does one think but in the mind?).

Recognizing that repetition sometimes serves a useful purpose, avoid repetition when it merely adds unnecessary words to the sentence.

27 Active and Passive Verbs

Consider whether an active verb would be preferable to a passive verb.

If the use of a passive verb is questionable, it is questionable stylistically, not grammatically. When we question the use of a passive verb, we are asking the writer to consider whether the sentence would not be more emphatic or more economical or less awkward or somehow "neater" if an active verb were used. Challenged to consider the options available in a particular sentence, the writer must be the final judge of the best choice in that case.

27

Sample revisions:

> **Original (1):** The additional entry **was listed** by our accountant as a justifiable and normal entry for a company that does not "underfund" the pension plan.

> **Revision:** Our accountant listed the additional entry as a normal and justifiable entry for a company that does not "underfund" the pension plan.

> **Original (2):** Because of the increasing use in automobiles of inflatable restraints (air bags), much testing **is required** of carmakers to ensure the correct and reliable operation of the system.

> **Revision:** Because of the increasing use in automobiles of inflatable restraints (air bags), carmakers must do a great deal of testing to ensure the correct and reliable operation of the system.

> **Original (3):** From these recurrent images of hard, resistant metals, it **can be inferred** by us that her husband is a mechanical, heartless person.

> **Revision:** From these recurrent images of hard, resistant metals, we can infer that her husband is a mechanical, heartless person.

Original (4): By asking a multitude of probing questions, she **was overwhelmed** by the government examiner.

Revision: By asking a multitude of probing questions, the government examiner **overwhelmed** her.

Explanation:

27

Writers sometimes decide to use the passive verb because they want to give special emphasis to some word in the sentence. In sentence 1, for instance, the words **additional entry** get special emphasis because they occupy the initial position. If an active verb is used in that sentence, however—as it is in the revision—the words **our accountant** get the special emphasis. The writer's choice of an active or passive verb in that sentence may depend on where he or she wants to put the emphasis.

It would be more difficult for the writers of sentences 2 and 3 to cite emphasis as the justification for their choices of the passive verb. Writers can also justify the use of the passive verb when they do not know the agent of the action or prefer not to reveal the agent or consider it unnecessary to indicate the agent, as in a sentence such as "The story was reported to all the newspapers."

Dangling verbals often result from the use of a passive verb in the main clause of a sentence (see also section 19). The context of sentence 4 suggests that the lead-off gerund phrase (**By asking ...**) may be dangling—that is, that it was not the woman (**she**) but the **government examiner** who was asking a multitude of questions. If the examiner was the questioner, the writer of that sentence may not choose the passive verb for the main clause but must use the active verb.

The use of a passive verb is *not* forbidden. But the writer should always be prepared to consider whether the use of a passive verb is justifiable or preferable in a particular sentence.

28 Correct, Exact, and Appropriate Words

Choose correct, exact, and appropriate words or expressions for what you intend to say. Avoid wrong words, faulty predications, and inexact words.

Wrong word:

28

A word is labeled *wrong* when it does not express the author's intended meaning. The most obvious instance of a "wrong word" is the substitution, usually due to carelessness, of a homonym (a like-sounding word) for the intended word; e.g. **through** for **threw**, **there** for **their**, **lose** for **loose**. Below you will find a list of commonly confused words and the page numbers where you may find their definition and usage in the glossary of usage or other places in this text.

Commonly Confused Words

accept, except (p. 226)

adverse, averse (p. 227)

advice, advise (p. 227)

affect, effect (p. 227)

all ready, already (p. 227)

all together, altogether (p. 228)

allusion, illusion (p. 227)

alot, a lot (p. 227)

any more, anymore (p. 228)

beside, besides (p. 228)

complement, compliment (p. 229)

continual, continuous (p. 229)

disinterested, uninterested (p. 230)

enthuse, enthused (p. 231)

farther, further (p. 231)

imply, infer (p. 232)

past, passed (p. 234)

principal, principle (p. 234)

their, there, they're (p. 236)

whose, who's (p. 237)

Sometimes, words are simply used in ways that make no sense given their meaning, as in the sentence that follows:

Original: As mentioned earlier, this method mimics the problem-solving techniques used by scientists, a desirable **trait** in any expert system.

Revision: As mentioned earlier, this method mimics the problem-solving techniques used by scientists, a desirable approach in any expert system.

In the appositive that ends this sentence, **a desirable trait in any expert system,** the writer has used the word **trait.** There is some ambiguity about whether the word **trait** is in apposition with **method** or **techniques,** but in either case, a **method** or a **technique** cannot be referred to as a **trait.** In the revision of this sentence, the word **approach** has been substituted for **trait.**

28

Sample revisions:

Original (1): Before we **dwell** deeply into the physics of laser beams, we need to review the most recent literature on the subject.

Revision: Before we **delve** deeply into the physics of laser beams, we need to review the most recent literature on the subject.

Original (2): We took the issue to the county **bored,** where the decision was overturned.

Revision: We took the issue to the county **board,** where the decision was overturned.

Original (3): Quality controls were allowed to lapse because these devices were never a problem for NASA until the tragic **assent** of the *Challenger.*

Revision: Quality controls were allowed to lapse because these devices were never a problem for NASA until the tragic **ascent** of the *Challenger.*

Original (4): We are under no obligation to give this aid to countries that are **quiet** capable of caring for themselves, to countries that make no effort to reduce population growth, or to countries where the aid is not likely to reduce starvation or malnutrition.

Revision: We are under no obligation to give this aid to countries that are **quite** capable of caring for themselves, to countries that make no effort to reduce population growth, or to countries where the aid is not likely to reduce starvation or malnutrition.

28

Faulty predication:

A faulty predication occurs when the verb or verb phrase doesn't "fit" logically with its subject.

Sample revisions:

Original (1): By adopting this system, the Parking Division would **receive less hassles** and more **appraisal.**

Revision: By adopting this system, the Parking Division would **experience fewer hassles** and gain more **approval.**

Original (2): This survey **does have justified criticisms.**

Revision: This survey **can be justifiably criticized.**

Original (3): This project **has high expectations** of success.

Revision: We confidently **expect** this project to succeed.

Original (4): An exemplary fuel system **is when** you get maximum efficiency at minimum cost.

Revision: An exemplary fuel system **is one** that provides maximum efficiency at minimum cost.

Original (5): The reason that she failed the examination **is because** she was sick at the time.

Revision: The reason she failed the examination **is that** she was sick at the time.

Original (6): The beach **is where** I get my worst sunburn.

Revision: The beach **is the place where** I get my worst sunburn.

Explanation:

In sentence 1, the verb **receive** is not compatible with both **hassles** and **appraisal.** We have substituted the verb **experience** to go with **hassles** and have used the verb **gain** to go with **appraisal.** But **appraisal** is also a wrong word here, and **less** is the wrong word to go with the countable noun **hassles.** So we have substituted **approval** for **appraisal** and **fewer** for **less.**

In sentence 2, because the verb **does have** is not a proper predication for the subject **survey,** we have changed the predicate to **can be justifiably criticized.** Likewise, in sentence 3, the predication **has high expectations** does not fit with the subject **project.** We have revised that sentence to read as follows: **We confidently expect this project to succeed.**

Sentences 4, 5, and 6 illustrate common instances of faulty predication involving a syntactical mismatch between the subject and the predicate. The adverb clauses in those sentences cannot serve as complements for the verb **to be.** (Nor could a simple adverb serve as the complement of the verb **to be:** "He is swiftly.") One way to revise such faulty predications is to put some kind of nominal structure after the **to be** verb: a noun, a noun phrase, or a noun clause. To avoid difficulties, it is best to avoid this kind of predication:

The reason is because . . .
An example is when . . .
A ghetto is where . . .

Inexact words:

Whereas a "wrong word" misses the target entirely by saying something other than what is intended, an "imprecise word" hits all around the bull's-eye and never on dead center by saying something close to what is meant but not quite accurate. The governing principle here is that we should strive only for as much precision in diction (word choice) as the situation demands.

In the spoken medium, diction is often imprecise. Fortunately, in many conversational situations, our diction does not have to be sharply precise in order to communicate adequately. In a conversation, for instance, if someone asked, "How did you like him?" we might respond, "Oh, I thought he was very nice." The word *nice* does not convey a precise meaning, but for the particular situation, it may be precise enough. The word *nice* here, reinforced by our tone of voice, certainly conveys the message that we approve of the person, that we are favorably disposed toward the person. In speech, we do not have the leisure to search for words that express our meaning exactly. If the person who asked the question were not satisfied with our general word of approval, *nice,* that person could ask us to be more specific about what we meant.

In the written medium, however, we do have the leisure to search for a precise word, and we are not available to the reader, who may want or need more specific information than our words supply. Generally, the written medium requires that the words we choose be as exact, as specific, and as unequivocal as we can make them. Consulting a thesaurus or, better yet, a dictionary that discriminates the meanings of synonyms will frequently yield the word that precisely conveys our intended meaning.

Sample revisions:

Original (1): I liked the movie *Presumed Innocent* because it was **interesting.**

Revision: I liked the movie *Presumed Innocent* because it was **suspenseful.**

Original (2): Integrity is a **thing** that everyone admires.

Revision: Integrity is a **virtue** that everyone admires.

Original (3): The corporation must do something about its **overwhelming ability** to lose money.

Revision: The corporation must do something about its **persistent tendency** to lose money.

Original (4): With the data gathered in my research, I will formulate a safety program that will **be more competent** than the one we now have.

Revision: With the data gathered in my research, I will formulate a safety program that will **be more reliable** than the one we now have.

28

Original (5): Most of this insurance money has been paid for **larger** accidents.

Revision: Most of this insurance money has been paid for **more serious** accidents.

Original (6): John cashed his government bonds, **as** he was about to go on his summer vacation.

Revision: John cashed his government bonds, **because** he was about to go on his summer vacation.

Explanation:

The word **interesting** in sentence 1 is too general to convey a precise meaning. A reader's response to such a general word would be to ask, "In what way was the movie interesting?" If the writer had written *exciting* or *thought-provoking* or *suspenseful*, readers might want more particulars, but at least they would have a clearer idea of the sense in which the writer of that sentence found the movie *interesting*.

In the oral medium, we can get by with a catchall word like **thing,** as in sentence 2, but writing allows us the leisure to search for a word that will serve as a more accurate predicate for **integrity.** We can choose a word like **policy, habit, disposition, virtue—**

whichever word fits best with what we want to say about integrity here.

The writer of sentence 3 may intend to be ironic when he or she speaks about **an overwhelming ability.** Both of the words in that phrase are positive, but losing money and being rated as a high risk by insurance companies are negative qualities. There would have been more of a matchup between the words and the qualities if the writer had used the phrase **its persistent tendency.** In sentence 4, **more reliable** would be a more exact predication to apply to **a safety program** than the phrase **more competent.** Likewise, in sentence 5, **catastrophic** or **serious** would be a more precise adjective to apply to **accidents** than the adjective **large.**

28

The subordinating conjunction **as** carries a variety of meanings, and it is not always possible to tell from the context which of its several meanings it carries in a particular sentence. In sentence 6, we cannot tell whether **as** is being used in its sense of "because" or "since" or "when" or "while." We should use the conjunction that exactly expresses our intended meaning: **when** he was about to go on his vacation or **because** he was about to go on his vacation—or whatever conjunction best says what we want to say. In the rewrite, we chose the subordinating conjunction **because.** Reserve the conjunction **as** for those contexts in which there is no possibility of ambiguity, as in sentences like "In that kind of situation, he acts exactly as he should" and "Do as I say."

Appropriate words:

A word is inappropriate if it does not fit—if it is out of tune with—the subject matter, the occasion, the audience, or the personality of the writer. It is a word that is conspicuously "out of place" in its environment.

No word in isolation can be labeled *inappropriate;* a word must be seen in the company of other words. Because technical writing often necessitates the use of specialized terminology, the diction in that kind of discourse may strike the uninitiated reader as being flagrantly inappropriate. But in the context of that kind of writing and for its audience, the jargon may very well be quite appropriate. What we are talking about in this section is the kind of word choice that is "out of place" in or "out of tune" with its context.

Sample revisions:

28

Original (1): He did not want to **exacerbate** his mother's **sangfroid,** so he **indicted** an **epistolary message** to inform her of his **unavoidable retardation.**

Revision: He did not want to **upset** his mother, so he **wrote** her a **note** to inform her that he would be **late.**

Original (2): Kids are frequently engaged in collaborative learning practices in this program.

Revision: Students are frequently engaged in collaborative learning practices in this program.

Original (3): The staff of the mayor's office were **freaked out** by the financial officer's budget report.

Revision: The staff of the mayor's office were **disconcerted** by the financial officer's budget report.

Original (4): These readings give us a **feel** for how precise the measuring system is.

Revision: These readings give us a **sense** of how precise the measuring system is.

Original (5): Whenever I visit New York City, I browse through at least one secondhand bookstore and eventually **cheapen** a book.

Revision: Whenever I visit New York City, I browse through at least one secondhand bookstore and eventually **bid for** a book.

Explanation:

Sentence 1 illustrates the kind of language used by writers when they are passing through a phase of learning a new discourse in which they seem unable to say even a simple thing in a simple way. While it is essential and admirable for developing writers to enlarge their vocabulary and expand their repertoire of rhetorical strategies, it is also important for them to learn to use a dictionary or thesaurus to check the accuracy of words and to consult other readers to test the appropriateness of words. When writers use too many polysyllabic words or use such words in ways they think will impress their readers rather than in ways they know they can express their ideas clearly, they run the risk of being labeled *pretentious*. To truly expand our working vocabulary, we must develop enough sophistication to be able to judge when language is appropriate and when it is not. As we develop that sophistication, we need to consciously "test" our choices against reference books and the judgment of other readers.

Sentences 2 and 3 exhibit the opposite kind of inappropriate language: language that is too colloquial for its occasion or audience. In sentence 3, **freaked out** is too colloquial for its context. **Disconcert,** the substitute verb for **freak out,** is not the kind of word that is part of most people's everyday vocabulary, especially in speech, but it is a word that fits in better with the surrounding words than the slang term does. Likewise, in sentence 2, the very common word **kids** does not fit well with the more formal level of diction established in the rest of the sentence. In sentence 4, the colloquial word **feel** is also out of tune with its environment. The word **sense** is more suitable for that context.

Sentence 5 illustrates another kind of inappropriateness. The word **cheapen** was once a perfectly appropriate word as used in this context. During the Elizabethan period in England (the sixteenth century), it was a common verb meaning "to bid for" or "to bargain for." If you look up the word in a modern dictionary, however, you will discover that **cheapen** in this sense is labeled *archaic*. The label

28

means that this word, in the sense of "to bargain for," can no longer be used in a modern context. While they are not archaic, many of the words that we use in the context of a particular discipline or discourse community may be used in other ways in other disciplines or discourse communities. Thus, it is wise to be sensitive to the particular ways in which words are used and to double-check the appropriateness of that usage in differing contexts.

Dictionaries, thesauruses, and handbooks can give you information about the denotation of words but not about the connotation of words. Thus, these resources cannot tell you precisely whether a word will be appropriate or not. You must finally rely on subject matter, occasion, audience, desired effect, and the character of your own personality to make reliable judgments about the appropriateness of your word choice. In general, keep in mind that your "voice" must remain in harmony with the overall tone that you have established in a particular piece of writing.

29

29 Correct Idioms

Use the proper idiom.

When we say that an expression is unidiomatic, we mean that native speakers of the language traditionally do not say it that way—in any dialect of the language. Editors or teachers can call your attention to an unidiomatic expression and can insert the correct idiom, but they often cannot give you rules or guidelines that will prevent other lapses in your use of the idiom. You simply have to learn the proper idioms by reading and listening attentively to the way the English language is written and spoken.

No word by itself is ever unidiomatic; only combinations of words can be unidiomatic. (For that reason, more than one word in the original sample sentences in the subsections below is **boldface.**)

Unidiomatic expressions:

Unidiomatic expressions are one of the most common weaknesses to be found in the prose of unpracticed writers. Why lapses of idiom occur so frequently is a good question, because writers presumably have not heard other native speakers use the curious expressions that they write down on paper. One explanation for the frequency of idiomatic lapses is that unpracticed writers use words and structures in the written medium that they seldom or never use in speech, and because they have not paid close enough attention to how something is said conventionally, they make a guess—usually a wrong guess—at how the expression should be phrased. Consider the sentence below:

29

> **Original: Had I didn't check** with the mathematics department about this course, I would have wasted both my time and my money.
>
> **Revision: Had I not checked** with the mathematics department about this course, I would have wasted both my time and my money.

The correct idiom here, **had I not checked,** is an alternative way of saying **if I had not checked.** The writer probably heard the **had** structure being used but did not remember how the expression was worded when she wrote the sentence.

Idioms involving prepositions:

Another of the most common idiomatic lapses involves a preposition in combination with some other word or words.

Sample revisions:

> **Original (1):** This report will **apprise you on** the suitability of the arboretum as the site of the trash-burning plant.
>
> **Revision:** This report will **apprise you of** the suitability of the arboretum as the site of the trash-burning plant.
>
> **Original (2):** There is no **point of** arguing with that person.

Revision: There is no **point in** arguing with that person.

Original (3): Our findings are **in accord to** the findings of the previous investigation.

Revision: Our findings are **in accord with** the findings of the previous investigation.

Original (4): Costell Corporation **differs with** the other members of the alliance in providing all service requirements to subsidiaries at cost.

Revision: Costell Corporation **differs from** the other members of the alliance in providing all service requirements to subsidiaries at cost.

Idioms involving infinitives:

1. The structure that fits idiomatically with the infinitive **to help** is not the participial structure **solving** but another infinitive structure, **[to] solve: to help you do, to help you arrange,** etc.

   Original: He was assigned to your company **to help you solving** some of your current problems.

   Revision: He was assigned to your company **to help you solve** some of your current problems.

2. Infinitive forms follow certain verbs conventionally.

AFTER . . . agree, ask, claim, decide, expect, have, hope, manage, offer, plan, pretend, say, wait, want, wish
USE . . . infinitive form (to + verb)

   Original: The investigative team **managed pulling** out the engines from the water within days of the crash.

   Revision: The investigative team **managed to pull** the engines out of the water within days of the crash.

Idioms involving articles or determiners:

The sentences below illustrate an idiomatic lapse that non-native-speakers often make: a lapse involving the use of the articles or determiners **the** and **a (an)**.

29

> **Original (1):** CSMP, which stands for "Continuous System Modeling Programs," **is program** that allows the operator to handle systems that are very complex.
>
> **Revision:** CSMP, which stands for "Continuous System Modeling Programs," **is a program** that allows the operator to handle systems that are very complex.
>
> **Original (2):** Make all checks payable **to university.**
>
> **Revision:** Make all checks payable **to the university.**
>
> **Original (3):** My daughter goes **to the college.**
>
> **Revision:** My daughter goes **to college.**

While it is reasonable to ask why we put the article **the** with the word **university** or **program** but leave it out with the word **college,** there is no rational explanation for the usages. We must simply commit them to memory.

Idioms involving gerunds:

Just as some verbs are followed by infinitives, so, too, are other verbs followed by gerunds conventionally.

AFTER . . . admit, appreciate, avoid, deny, discuss, enjoy, finish, imagine, miss, quit, recall, resist, suggest
USE . . . gerund form (verb + -ing)

Original: Lasers **finish to make** the intricate designs on each custom-ordered piece.

Revision: Lasers **finish making** the intricate designs on each custom-ordered piece.

30 Trite or Overused Expressions

30

Avoid trite expressions.

Trite expressions are certain combinations of words or certain figures of speech that have been used so often that they have lost their freshness and even their meaning for most readers. Rhetorically, the price you pay for using trite language is the alienation of your readers. Readers stop paying attention. You may have something new and important to say, but if your message is delivered in threadbare language, you will lose or fail to capture the attention of your readers.

There is nothing grammatically or idiomatically wrong with a trite expression. A trite expression is only *stylistically* objectionable—mainly because it is a *tired* expression.

Sample revisions:

Original (1): When we finished our research, we were **tired but happy.**

Revision: When we finished our research, we were **exhausted but content.**

Original (2): Convinced that the use of drugs has increased dramatically among the workers, this company must **nip the problem in the bud** before it **runs rampant.**

Revision: Convinced that the use of drugs has increased dramatically among the workers, this company must **solve the problem** before it **gets out of control.**

Original (3): She didn't **bat an eyelash** when I told her **flat out** that she **was born with a silver spoon in her mouth.**

Revision: She didn't **squirm a bit** when I told her **frankly** that she **was a pampered child.**

30

Figures of speech are especially prone to staleness. Metaphors like **nip in the bud** were once fresh and cogent; now they are so wilted from overuse that we call them *dead metaphors.* Similarly, combinations of words like **tired but happy** and **runs rampant** now produce glazed-eyed readers. Other trite expressions have been uttered so often that they have become folk expressions. Every generation picks up tired expressions like the following: **the apple of one's eye, waited with bated breath, taking it on the chin, eat your heart out, one foot in the grave, in cold blood, knee-jerk response, chip on one's shoulder,** and **toe the mark.**

Ironically, one of the ways in which to revise sentences that include trite language is to use the most familiar, ordinary language. Sentence 1, for instance, is improved simply by the use of different words for the expression **tired but happy.** If you make an effort to invent your own figures of speech, you may produce awkward, strained figures, but at least they will be fresh. Instead of adopting the hackneyed metaphor **nip in the bud,** make up your own metaphor, such as the one in the following sentence:

Convinced that the use of drugs has increased dramatically among workers, our company must excise this tumor before it becomes a raging cancer.

Reading a great deal yourself and having others read your prose will help you to develop an eye for trite expressions. Be wary of weary words.

31 Mixed Metaphors

Avoid mixed metaphors.

A metaphor is one of several types of *figurative language,* language that creates in our minds an image of a concept or relationship, enabling us to understand that concept or relationship clearly and creatively. Because they treat two seemingly different items as one and the same thing, metaphors allow writers to make both engaging and clear comparisons. To be effective, however, metaphors need to contain elements that are indeed comparable in the way that the metaphor suggests.

31

A mixed metaphor is the result of a writer's failure to keep a consistent image in mind. All metaphors are based on perceived likenesses between things that exist in different orders of being; for instance, between a man and a greyhound ("The lean shortstop is a greyhound when he runs the bases"), fame and a spur ("Fame is the spur to ambition"), mail and an avalanche ("The mail buried the staff under an avalanche of complaints"). Whenever any detail is incompatible with one or more terms of the analogy, the metaphor is said to be mixed.

Sample revisions:

> **Original (1):** When we tried to get our proposal **off the ground,** we found that it **sank in a sea of apathy.**
>
> **Revision:** When we tried to get our proposal **off the ground,** we found that it **did not get up enough speed to become airborne.**
>
> or
>
> When we tried to **set sail with our proposal,** we found that it **sank in a sea of apathy.**
>
> **Original (2):** In "The Dead," James Joyce uses small talk as **an effective weapon to illustrate** his thesis.

Revision: In "The Dead," James Joyce uses small talk as **an effective mirror to reflect** his thesis.

Original (3): The extraordinary success of this project struck **a spark that massaged** the team's enthusiasm.

Revision: The extraordinary success of this project struck **a spark that ignited** the team's enthusiasm.

31

Original (4): The manager tried **to scale the wall** of their indifference but found that he could not **burrow** through it.

Revision: The manager tried **to scale the wall** of their indifference but found that he could not **surmount** it.

Original (5): When his mother saw that he was ready **to fly off the handle,** she made him **toe the mark.**

Revision: When his mother saw that he was ready **to fly off the handle,** she forced him **to obey her rules.**

Explanation:

In sentence 1 above, the image that is begun in the first part of the sentence cannot be sustained in the second part: a plane takes off; then a ship sinks. Similarly, if one were scaling a wall, one could not at the same time be digging through it (sentence 4). A spark can start a fire but not massage anything (sentence 3). Neither could a weapon illustrate (sentence 2).

In section 30 on trite expressions, we spoke about the staleness of "dead metaphors." Sentence 5 presents an example of two dead metaphors that are incompatible when used together (**fly off the handle,** alluding to an ax flying off its handle, and **toe the mark,** an expression from foot racing). To avoid the mixture of metaphors in that sentence, we resorted to a literal rather than a figurative expression in the latter half of the sentence: **to obey her rules.** Figures of speech such as metaphors lend color and vivacity to your style, and for that reason, you should cultivate their use. But remember that when you resort to poetic analogies, forming and maintaining a clear picture of the notion you are attempting to express figuratively will ensure a consistent metaphor.

32 Biased or Sexist Language

32

Avoid language that may offend readers because it reflects bias, sexism, or stereotyping.

Language use is constantly—though sometimes subtly—modified by expanding vocabulary, evolving conceptualizations, common usage, and social change. In the past few decades, social sensitivity to bias or prejudice with regard to gender, race, ethnicity, or religion has led to several universally recognized changes in conventional language use. While there are as yet no formal rules for unbiased usage, the following suggestions can help you avoid potential offense to your readers.

1. Use gender-specific pronouns only where appropriate:

> Stephen Hawking views most of **his** works as contributions to the development of a unified theory of physical phenomena.

Refer to people in general by using plural noun forms, eliminating pronouns altogether, or using **he or she** (**him or her**).

> **Original:** According to Hawking, **a scientist** needs to work toward taking **his** partial theories on relativity and quantum mechanics and unifying them into a single comprehensive explanation of physics.

Revision: According to Hawking, **scientists** need to work toward unifying **their** partial theories on relativity and quantum mechanics into a single comprehensive explanation of physics.

or

According to Hawking, **a scientist** needs to work toward unifying **his or her** partial theories on relativity and quantum mechanics into a single comprehensive explanation of physics.

32

2. Avoid using the word **man** or a word form containing **man** to refer to people in general.

Original: That's one small step for **man,** one giant leap for **mankind.**

Revision: That's one small step for **a human being,** one giant leap for **humanity.**

Original: In this survey, low voter turnout seems to have a direct correlation to the belief that **congressmen** vote more from their own convictions, prompting from lobbyists, and political bargaining than from their sensitivity to the voting constituency.

Revision: In this survey, low voter turnout seems to have a direct correlation to the belief that **members of Congress** vote more from their own convictions, prompting from lobbyists, and political bargaining than from their sensitivity to the voting constituency.

3. Avoid gendered stereotypes or patronizing references.

Original: In the hearings, **stewardesses** complained of extended flight hours, malfunctioning equipment, and insufficient time for cabin checks.

Revision: In the hearings, **flight attendants** complained of extended flight hours, malfunctioning equipment, and insufficient time for cabin checks.

4. Use ethnic or racial references that are currently conventional and acceptable.

Use . . . Native American	instead of . . . Indian
Use . . . African-American	instead of . . . black
Use . . . Asian	instead of . . . Oriental

Punctuation and Mechanics

Most writers who are using a handbook like this one as a quick reference guide become frustrated by a textual format that separates punctuation from mechanics. They are concerned more with where to locate conventions governing the use of a particular graphic device than with technical distinctions among devices of language. For that reason, we treat conventions of punctuation and mechanics together in this section of the text. However, to accommodate those readers who do need or want to know more about the distinctions between these two features of written language, we maintain separate discussions of punctuation and mechanics in the introduction which follows.

Punctuation:

Graphic punctuation performs the kinds of functions that intonation (**pitch, stress, pause, and juncture**) performs in spoken language. Punctuation and intonation can be considered a part of the grammar of the language because they join with other grammatical devices (**word order, inflections, and function words**) to help convey meaning. As writers experience how punctuation functions as an integral—and often indispensable—part of the expressive system of a language, they cease to think of it as just another nuisance imposed on them by editors and English teachers and become far more careful and deliberate with its use. The general principles governing the use of punctuation marks are sketched out in the table that follows.

Four Main Functions of Punctuation

For *linking* parts of sentences and words:

semicolon ; (see pp. 122–125)
colon : (see pp. 125–128)
dash — (see pp. 129–131)
hyphen (for words only) - (see pp. 147–151)

For *separating* sentences and parts of sentences:

period . (see pp. 133–135)
question mark ? (see pp. 134–135)
exclamation point ! (see pp. 134–135)
comma , (see pp. 106–121)

For *enclosing* parts of sentences:

pair of commas , . . . , (see pp. 113–114, 117–119, 131–133)
pair of dashes — . . . — (see pp. 131–133)
pair of parentheses (. . .) (see pp. 131–133)
pair of brackets [. . .]
pair of quotation marks " . . . " (see pp. 133–137)

For *indicating* omissions:

apostrophe (e.g., **don't, we'll, it's, we've**) (see pp. 103–106)
period (e.g., abbreviations: **Mrs., U.S., A. H. Robinson**)
dash (e.g., **John R—, D—n!**)
triple periods (. . . to indicate omitted words in a quotation)

Mechanics:

Graphic devices such as **quotation marks, underlining, italics, hyphens, numbers,** and **capitalization** are sometimes classified as punctuation. But because such graphic devices are not correlated—as punctuation marks are—with the intonation patterns of the spoken language, these devices are often grouped under a separate heading called *mechanics*. In the spoken language, a word printed with an initial capital letter is pronounced no differently from the same word printed with an initial lowercase letter. Nor is the italicized or underlined title of a book pronounced any differently from that same title printed without italics. (However, the use of italics or underlining to indicate that a word or phrase should be emphasized does correspond to stress in the spoken language.) Even quotation marks, which we might regard as correlated with the spoken language, do not correspond to anything the voice does when it creates direct speech. Because of their slightly different character, then, these graphic devices are often placed in a category of their own.

33

Conventional use of punctuation and mechanics:

In use, whether we classify graphic devices as punctuation or mechanics is immaterial. What is important to remember is that all of the devices discussed in this section of the handbook are part of written language exclusively and that they facilitate the reading of that language. Most readers would have at least momentary difficulty making sense of the following string of words:

> Jill cried buckets as many as you can fetch Jack thought I don't have to please you over there she continued nuts pails they're called yelled Jack.

But if the proper punctuation and mechanics were used with that string of words, readers would be spared any difficulty in trying to decipher the flow:

> Jill cried, "Buckets! As many as you can fetch!" Jack thought, "I don't have to!" "Please, you over there!" she continued. "Nuts! *Pails* they're called!" yelled Jack.

Without the resources of the human voice to clarify the meaning of their words as spoken, writers depend on typographical devices to help their readers understand the nuances of what they are trying to say.

Punctuation and mechanics are strictly conventions. While it is important to follow the conventions that have been established in order to help readers make meaning, there is no *reason* in the nature of things why the mark ? has to be used in the English language to indicate a question. The classical Greek language, for instance, used the mark ; (what we call the *semicolon*) to indicate questions. Nor is there any reason in the nature of things why the comma should be a separating device rather than a linking device. Nor is there a particular reason why some titles are underlined and others are put in quotation marks rather than the other way around. It is usage that has established the distinctive functions of the various marks. (As a matter of fact, it was printers, not grammarians, who created the various marks of punctuation.)

Although publishers of newspapers, magazines, and books often have style manuals that prescribe, for their own editors and writers, a style of punctuation that may differ in some particulars from the prevailing conventions, writers who observe the conventions set forth in this section can rest assured that they are conforming to the predominant system used in the United States.

33 Apostrophe Shows Possession

Use an apostrophe for the possessive case of the noun.

$$\boxed{\text{noun}}\ \text{'s}\ \boxed{\text{noun}}\ \text{s'}$$

poet's   poets'

Here are the basic guidelines for forming the possessive case of the English noun.

Guidelines for forming the possessive case of nouns:

1. Most English nouns form the possessive case with **'s** (singular) or **s'** (plural):

   book's cover (singular), **books' covers** (plural)

   An alternative form = *of* phrase:

   the commands of the general (instead of **the general's commands**)

33

2. Nouns that form their plural in ways other than by adding an -s form their possessive plural by adding **'s** to the plural of the noun:

   woman's/women's, man's/men's, child's/children's, ox's/oxen's, deer's/deer's, mouse's/mice's

3. Some writers simply add an apostrophe to form the possessive case of singular nouns ending in -s:

   the goddess' fame
   the alumnus' contribution
   Keats' odes
   Dickens' novels

   Alternative form = add the usual **'s** to form the possessive case of such nouns:

   goddess's, alumnus's (plural: **alumni's**), **Keats's, Dickens's**

   Take your choice, but be consistent.

4. Form the possessive case of *pairs* of nouns as follows:
   To show *joint* possession: add **'s** only to the second member of the pair:

   John and Mary's mother, the brothers and sister's car

   To show *individual* possession: add **'s** to each member of the pair

   the boy's and girl's bedrooms, John's and Mary's tennis rackets, the men's and women's locker rooms

5. Form the possessive case of group nouns or compound nouns by adding 's to the end of the unit:

   commander in chief's, someone else's, president-elect's, editor in chief's, son-in-law's

   If compounds form their plural by adding -s to the first word, form the possessive case by adding 's to the end of the unit:

   editors in chief's, sons-in-law's

6. Normally reserve the 's or s' for the possessive case of nouns naming animate creatures (human beings and animals). The **of** phrase is more commonly used for the possessive of inanimate nouns:

   the roof of the house (instead of **the house's roof**)

   Exceptions: Usage now sanctions the use of 's with some common inanimate nouns:

   a day's wages, a week's work, the year's death toll, the school's policies, the car's performance, the radio's tone

34 Possessive Pronoun *its* and Contraction *it's*

Its is the possessive case of the pronoun *it*; *it's* is the contraction of *it is* or *it has*.

More mistakes have been made with the pronoun **it** than with any other single word in the English language. The mistakes result from confusion about the two -s forms of this pronoun. **It's** is often used where **its** is the correct form (**The dog broke it's leg** instead of the correct form, **The dog broke its leg**), and **its** is often used where **it's** is the correct form (**Its a shame that the girl broke her leg** instead of the correct form, **It's a shame that the girl broke her leg**).

If you use **it's** for the possessive case of **it,** you are probably influenced by the 's that is used to form the possessive case of the singular noun (e.g., **the man's hat**). You might be helped to avoid this mistake if you kept in mind that *none of the personal pronouns uses 's to form its possessive case:* I/my, you/your, he/his, she/her, it/its, we/our, they/their. So you should write, **The company lost its lease.**

You might also be helped to avoid this mistake if you remembered that the apostrophe has another function in written English: to indicate the omission of one or more letters in an English word, as in contractions (**I'll, don't, she'd**). The apostrophe in the word **it's** signals the contraction of the expression **it is** or **it has.** So you should write, **It's the first loss that the company has suffered** or **It's come to my attention that you are frequently late.**

Don't let this little word defeat you.

35 Comma in Compound Sentences

Put a comma in front of the coordinating conjunction that joins the independent clauses of a compound sentence.

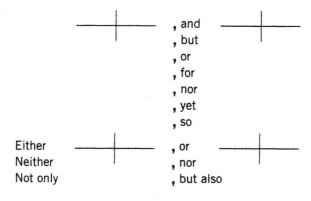

This convention of the comma comes into play only in compound sentences (sentences composed of two or more independent clauses) or in compound-complex sentences (sentences composed of two or more independent clauses and at least one dependent clause). According to section 37, pairs of words, phrases, or clauses (except independent clauses) joined by one of the coordinating conjunctions should not be separated with a comma.

35

Sample revisions:

Original (1): The purpose of the letter is evident and the organization of the letter is excellent.

Revision: The purpose of the letter is evident, and the organization of the letter is excellent.

Original (2): We must attract more qualified people into the nursing profession or we will face both short-term and long-term consequences.

Revision: We must attract more qualified people into the nursing profession, or we will face both short-term and long-term consequences.

Original (3): Johann Strauss composed hundreds of dances over the years but his art remained fresh and young.

Revision: Johann Strauss composed hundreds of dances over the years, but his art remained fresh and young.

Original (4): They resented this kind of treatment yet they agreed to sign the contract.

Revision: They resented this kind of treatment, yet they agreed to sign the contract.

Original (5): He officiated at the funeral for his mother requested he do so.

Revision: He officiated at the funeral, for his mother requested he do so.

Original (6): Either the president will veto the bill or the Supreme Court will rule that the bill is unconstitutional.

35

Revision: Either the president will veto the bill, or the Supreme Court will rule that the bill is unconstitutional.

Explanation:

This practice of using a comma probably developed because in many compound sentences, the absence of a comma could lead to an initial misreading of the sentence. In sentence 5, for instance, it would be quite natural for us to read **for** as a preposition and consequently to read the sentence this way:

He officiated at the funeral for his mother . . .

But when we came to the verb **requested,** we would realize that we had misread the sentence, and we would have to go back and reread it.

Some handbooks suggest that it is acceptable to omit this separating comma under certain conditions. However, if you *always* insert a comma before the coordinating conjunction that joins independent clauses, you never have to pause to consider whether these conditions are present, and you can be confident that your sentence will always be read correctly the first time. The safest practice is *always* to insert the comma before the coordinating conjunction or before the second of the correlative conjunctions (**either . . . or; neither . . . nor; not only . . . but also**) that join the main clauses of a compound or compound-complex sentence.

36 Commas with Introductory Words, Phrases, or Clauses

Introductory words, phrases, or clauses should be separated from the main (independent) clause by a comma.

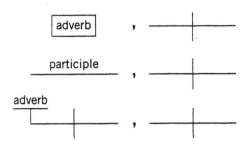

36

The reason for the commas after introductory elements is that the comma facilitates the reading of the sentence and often prevents an initial misreading of it. Without the "protective" comma, the syntax of the sentence structures can be misunderstood, as in the sentence that follows:

> Besides the crowd was not impressed by his flaming oratory.

Should we pause for emphasis in our reading after the phrase *Besides the crowd* or after the word *besides*? If you always insert a comma after an introductory word, phrase, or clause, you will not have to consider whether it is safe to omit the comma. Your readers will be less likely to experience false starts in their reading.

Sample revisions:

> **Original (1):** Before the executives depended on a committee of engineers to advise them.

> **Revision:** Before, the executives depended on a committee of engineers to advise them.

Original (2): In both positions I have recommended that employees be adequately insured before they are permitted to undertake the job.

Revision: In both positions, I have recommended that employees be adequately insured before they are permitted to undertake the job.

Original (3): Although she vehemently protested the violence was not as destructive as she had predicted it would be.

36

Revision: Although she vehemently protested, the violence was not as destructive as she had predicted it would be.

Original (4): If uncorrected faulty reasoning can lead to unsound or unproductive practices in science.

Revision: If uncorrected, faulty reasoning can lead to unsound or unproductive practices in science.

Original (5): Getting further information about enrollment in the program I requested a tour of duty with my friends on the medical team in Guatemala.

Revision: Getting further information about enrollment in the program, I requested a tour of duty with my friends on the medical team in Guatemala.

Original (6): After a few years time away from work seemed to be more important to the employees than did the overtime pay.

Revision: After a few years, time away from work seemed to be more important to the employees than did the overtime pay.

Explanation:

If we had not revised the sentences above by using an introductory comma, some readers would probably have read the sentences this way the first time:

1. Before the executives depended on a committee of engineers . . .
2. In both positions I have recommended . . .

3. Although she vehemently protested the violence . . .
4. If uncorrected faulty reasoning can lead to unsound or unproductive practices . . .
5. Getting further information about enrollment in the program I requested . . .
6. After a few years' time . . .

The insertion of a comma after each of these introductory elements prevented even the possibility of that kind of misreading.

37

37 Don't Use Commas to Join Pairs

Pairs of words, phrases, or dependent clauses joined by one of the coordinating conjunctions should not be separated with a comma. (See p. 113 for exceptions to this convention.)

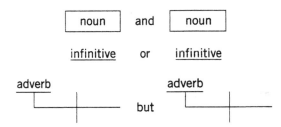

The principle behind this convention is that what has been *joined* by one means (the coordinating conjunction) should not then be *separated* by another means (the comma, a separating device). The purpose of the coordinating conjunction (*and, but, or, nor*) is to join units of equal rank (e.g., nouns with nouns, verbs with verbs, prepositional phrases with prepositional phrases, adjective clauses with adjective clauses). Once pairs of coordinate units have been joined by the conjunction, it makes no sense to separate them with a comma— as has been done in all the examples which follow.

Sample revisions:

Original (1): These theoretical computations do not take into consideration wind speed, or temperature variations. **(two noun phrases joined by *or*)**

Revision: These theoretical computations do not take into consideration wind speed or temperature variations.

37

Original (2): The response of the language experts to these changes is skeptical, and even predictable. **(two adjectives joined by *and*)**

Revision: The response of the language experts to these changes is skeptical and even predictable.

Original (3): Most of the students are not equally prepared for higher education, and don't fit into the "box" of expectations established by the Admissions Office. **(two verb phrases joined by *and*)**

Revision: Most of the students are not equally prepared for higher education and don't fit into the "box" of expectations established by the Admissions Office.

Original (4): French author Jean Baudrillard suggests that evil is not at all undesirable, and that it is even necessary to the vitality of humankind. **(two noun clauses joined by *and*)**

Revision: French author Jean Baudrillard suggests that evil is not at all undesirable and that it is even necessary to the vitality of humankind.

Original (5): Students avoid signing up for late-afternoon classes not because they can concentrate better in the morning, but because they have to go to work in the afternoon. **(two adverb clauses joined by *but*)**

Revision: Students avoid signing up for late-afternoon classes not because they can concentrate better in the morning but because they have to go to work in the afternoon.

Original (6): Two assistants record data that will determine the maximum altitude of the model rocket, or the time it takes for the ping-pong balls to return to the ground. **(two nouns [*altitude, time*] joined by *or*)**

Revision: Two assistants record data that will determine the maximum altitude of the model rocket or the time it takes for the ping-pong balls to return to the ground.

37

☞ Note

A pair of *independent* clauses does not come under this rule. According to Section 35, a comma should be inserted before the coordinating conjunction, because in this structure, the omission of the comma could lead—and often does lead—to an initial misreading of the sentence; e.g., **The *Bulls won* the game, and *Chicago celebrated* a fourth championship season.**

Exceptions:

An exception to the convention of not using commas to separate pairs that have been joined occurs in the case of suspended structures, as in the following sentences:

The report about the biologist's struggle with, and triumph over, numerous obstacles fascinated me.

We must never relinquish our interest in, and respect for, the accomplishments of our ancestors.

The phrases **struggle with** and **triumph over** are called *suspended structures* because they are "left hanging" until they are completed by the noun phrase **numerous obstacles.** Likewise, the phrases **interest in** and **respect for** are "suspended" until they are completed by the phrase **the accomplishments of our ancestors.**

Another exception to this convention occurs in the structure where the word or phrase following the first word or phrase presents not an alternative to the previous word or phrase (as in "right or wrong" and "apples and oranges") but an *explanatory appositive* for the previous word or phrase. In such cases, the explanatory appositive is enclosed within a pair of commas, as in the following example:

> The holograph, or handwritten manuscript, was carefully examined by archaeologists.

38

With these two exceptions, the joining device (the conjunction) and the separating device (the comma) should not work against each other.

38 Commas Separate Items in a Series

Use a comma to separate a series of coordinate words, phrases, or clauses.

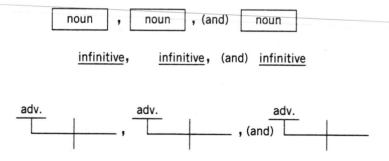

(The parentheses around **and** in the diagrams indicate that the coordinating conjunction between the last two members of a series may sometimes be dispensed with; e.g., **The tall, robust, gray-haired soldier rose to speak** is stylistically preferable to **The tall, robust, and gray-haired soldier rose to speak.**)

Whereas, conventionally, pairs of coordinate words, phrases, or clauses are not separated by a comma, a series (three or more) of coordinate words, phrases, or clauses should be separated by commas.

> Artists with formidable **skills, originality, and determination** are often not employed in their domain of talent because that talent is unneeded or unappreciated by society. **(series of nouns)**

It has become acceptable to omit the comma between the last two members of the series when they are joined by a coordinating conjunction. However, this option sometimes leads to ambiguity, as in the following sentence:

38

> He appealed to the management, the presidents and the vice presidents.

In this sentence, it is not clear whether he appealed to three different groups (**management, presidents, vice presidents**)—a meaning that would have been clearly indicated by the **a, b, and c** formula—or only to one group, **management,** who are then specified in two appositives, **presidents** and **vice presidents.** Since there is never any chance of ambiguity if you invariably use the **a, b, and c** formula, you will find this option the safest one.

Sample revisions:

> **Original (1):** Some of the tactics they have adopted for dealing with the parking problem are arriving very early incessantly circling the parking lot parking on nearby streets and even changing their residence so that they can walk to work. **(series of gerund phrases)**

> **Revision:** Some of the tactics they have adopted for dealing with the parking problem are arriving very early, incessantly circling the parking lot, parking on nearby streets, and even changing their residence so that they can walk to work.

> **Original (2):** The Board of Directors declared that they are developing a system of fines for first-time vandalism that they will be

raising house dues to cover recent damages and that they will ban repeat offenders from residing in the house. **(series of noun clauses)**

Revision: The Board of Directors declared that they are developing a system of fines for first-time vandalism, that they will be raising house dues to cover recent damages, and that they will ban repeat offenders from residing in the house.

Original (3): Four techniques commonly used in the sciences are analysis classification definition and description. **(series of nouns)**

38

Revision: Four techniques commonly used in the sciences are analysis, classification, definition, and description.

Original (4): Our task is to arrest the pollution alleviate the discomfort of the inhabitants and discover the cause of the contamination. **(series of verb phrases)**

Revision: Our task is to arrest the pollution, alleviate the discomfort of the inhabitants, and discover the cause of the contamination.

Original (5): My father was distracted by the stresses of medical school my mother was consumed with being the family breadwinner and my grandmother was left to tend all of the children. **(series of independent clauses)**

Revision: My father was distracted by the stresses of medical school, my mother was consumed with being the family bread-winner, and my grandmother was left to tend all of the children.

☞ Note

Built on the principle of parallelism (see section 25), a series always involves words, phrases, or clauses of a similar kind. So a series should never couple dissimilar grammatical elements; for example, nouns with adjectives, prepositional phrases with infinitive phrases, or adjective clauses with adverb clauses.

39 Commas Set Off Nonrestrictive Clauses

Nonrestrictive adjective clauses should be enclosed with a pair of commas.

A nonrestrictive adjective clause is one that supplies additional information about the noun it modifies but information that is not needed to identify or specify the particular person, place, or thing that is being talked about. Conventionally, these clauses are marked off with commas.

39

Punctuating Nonrestrictive Adjective Clauses

Identify the clause: This plant deals only with rural stores *which are normally closed during winter months.*

IF: the particular person, place, or thing being talked about (e.g., rural stores) is sufficiently identified by what is left (e.g., **This plant deals only with rural stores**)

THEN: the clause can be considered nonrestrictive, and we mark it off with commas.

This plant deals only with rural stores, which are normally closed during winter months.

In writing, it makes a significant difference whether the adjective clause in a sentence is marked off or not. *With* the comma, the sentence above means that the plant deals exclusively with rural stores (which, incidentally, are usually closed during winter months). *Without* the comma, this sentence means that the plant deals exclusively with rural stores that are closed during the winter months (in other words, the plant does not deal at all with those rural stores that are *open* during winter months). Those two meanings are quite different from each other.

Instances in Which Adjective Clauses Are Almost Always Nonrestrictive

39

1. Where the antecedent is a **proper noun,** the adjective clause is usually nonrestrictive:

   New York City, which has the largest urban population in the United States, . . .

   The College of William and Mary, which was founded in 1693, . . .

2. Where, in the nature of things, there could be **only one such** person, place, or thing, the adjective clause is usually nonrestrictive:

   My mother, who is now forty-six years old, . . .

   His fingerprints, which are on file in Washington, . . .

3. Where the identity of the antecedent has been clearly established by the **previous context,** the adjective clause is usually nonrestrictive:

   The plant, which is now 84 years old, . . . **(where the previous sentence has identified the particular plant being talked about)**

   Such revolutions, which never enlist the sympathies of the majority of the people, . . . **(where the kinds of revolutions being talked about have been specified in the previous sentences or paragraphs)**

Writers usually use **which** to introduce nonrestrictive adjective clauses referring to nonhuman nouns and **who (whose, whom)** to introduce nonrestrictive adjective clauses referring to humans. For more information about the use of **which** and **who** as relative pronouns introducing nonrestrictive clauses, see section 20.

Sample revisions:

Original (1): My partner waved to his wife whom he spotted as soon as we entered the stadium.

Revision: My partner waved to his wife, whom he spotted as soon as we entered the stadium.

Original (2): Time management which has four distinct but related phases is an important aspect of corporate culture.

Revision: Time management, which has four distinct but related phases, is an important aspect of corporate culture.

40

Original (3): His oldest brother who is a physicist is the chief of staff at Rockwell International.

Revision: His oldest brother, who is a physicist, is the chief of staff at Rockwell International.

Original (4): Hubbard Laboratories, Inc. which has 45 million shares traded on the New York Stock Exchange engages in manufacturing and marketing pharmaceutical drugs.

Revision: Hubbard Laboratories, Inc., which has 45 million shares traded on the New York Stock Exchange, engages in manufacturing and marketing pharmaceutical drugs.

40 Don't Use Commas in Restrictive Clauses

Restrictive adjective clauses should not be marked off with a pair of commas.

A restrictive adjective clause is one that is essential in identifying or specifying the particular person, place, or thing being talked about. It "restricts" or "defines"—that is, it "draws boundaries around"— the noun being talked about.

Testing for Restrictive Adjective Clauses

40

Identify the clause:

All employees *who enroll in the PPO option* are entitled to $5.00 copay prescriptions.

IF: the clause is essential to identifying the noun it modifies (e.g., if *only those enrolled in the PPO* get the $5.00 copay)

THEN: the clause is restrictive, and we do not use commas to mark it off.

All employees who enroll in the PPO option are entitled to $5.00 copay prescriptions.

Sample revisions:

Original (1): All children, **who were in the front row,** received free ice cream.

Revision: All children **who were in the front row** received free ice cream.

Original (2): This information should include a map, **that specifies the areas where it is permissible to park.**

Revision: This information should include a map **that specifies the areas where it is permissible to park.**

Original (3): Middle-aged operators, **who have slow reflexes,** should not handle high-speed machinery.

Revision: Middle-aged operators **who have slow reflexes** should not handle high-speed machinery.

Original (4): All streets, alleys, and thoroughfares, **which are in the public domain,** should be maintained by the city.

Revision: All streets, alleys, and thoroughfares **that are in the public domain** should be maintained by the city.

Original (5): Clinical studies established that women, **who took DES,** were at an increased risk of developing vaginal cancer.

40

Revision: Clinical studies established that women **who took DES** were at an increased risk of developing vaginal cancer.

Explanation:

In sentence 1, the adjective clause **who were in the first row** is restrictive because it identifies, defines, designates, and specifies *which* children received free ice cream. The writer of that sentence did not intend to say that *all* children received free ice cream, but with commas enclosing that adjective clause, the sentence does suggest that all of them received free ice cream. According to convention, if the writer wishes to say that *only the children who were in the first row* received free ice cream, that identifying **who** clause cannot be enclosed in commas; it must stand unseparated from the noun that it helps to identify. Similarly, if we revise sentences 2, 3, 4, and 5 by omitting the commas, the sentences will say what the writers intended them to say.

Restrictive adjective clauses modifying nonhuman nouns should be introduced with the relative pronoun **that;** restrictive adjective clauses modifying human nouns should be introduced with the relative pronoun **who.** For more information about the appropriate use of the relative pronouns **that, who,** and **which** and information about occasions when relative pronouns may be omitted, see section 20.

41 Semicolons in Compound Sentences

If the independent clauses of a compound sentence are not joined by one of the coordinating conjunctions, they should be joined by a semicolon.

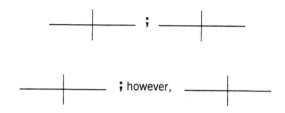

As pointed out in section 35, the coordinating conjunctions are **and, but, or, for, nor, yet,** and **so.** In the absence of one of those words, the independent clauses of a compound sentence should be spliced together with a punctuation device: the semicolon.

Words and phrases such as **however, therefore, then, indeed, moreover, thus, nevertheless, consequently, furthermore, in fact, on the other hand,** and **on the contrary** are not coordinating conjunctions; they are called *conjunctive adverbs*. Conjunctive adverbs provide logical links between sentences and parts of sentences, but they do not function as grammatical splices. Unlike coordinating conjunctions, which must always be placed between the two elements they join, conjunctive adverbs enjoy some freedom of movement in the sentence.

Sample revisions:

Original (1): The court sought to enforce its subpoena of the records from the counselor's internal investigation, **however,** it did not order the counselor to comply with the subpoena.

Revision: The court sought to enforce its subpoena of the records from the counselor's internal investigation; **however,** it did not order the counselor to comply with the subpoena.

Original (2): Your supervisor requested only a report that tallies how many employees attended each program, **nevertheless,** you know that there is more to the evaluation. What will you do?

Revision: Your supervisor requested only a report that tallies how many employees attended each program; **nevertheless,** you know that there is more to the evaluation. What will you do?

Original (3): We maintained a computerized storage system for two years, **later,** we established a highly sophisticated retrieval system.

41

Revision: We maintained a computerized storage system for two years; **later,** we established a highly sophisticated retrieval system.

Original (4): To arrest this expensive loss of heat, you should insulate your house, **in fact,** it would be advisable for you to install this insulation as soon as possible.

Revision: To arrest this expensive loss of heat, you should insulate your house; **in fact,** it would be advisable for you to install this insulation as soon as possible.

Original (5): As shown in Figure 2, there are several irregular surges of voltage during the test; **proving that the safety devices designed for this project have not yet been perfected.**

Revision: As shown in Figure 2, there are several irregular surges of voltage during the test; **these irregular surges prove that the safety devices designed for this project have not yet been perfected.**

Explanation:

In sentence 1, the word **however** is placed between two independent clauses, but evidence that this conjunctive adverb is not serving as the grammatical splicer of the two clauses is provided by the fact that **however** can be shifted to another position in the sentence: **The court sought to enforce its subpoena of the records from the counselor's internal investigation; it did not, however, order the counselor to comply with the subpoena.** The coordinating conjunction **but,** on the other hand, which is equivalent to **however,** could occupy no other position in the sentence than between the end of the first clause (after the word **investigation**) and the beginning of the next clause (before the word **it**).

Nor can the independent clauses of a compound sentence be joined by a comma, because the comma is a separating device, not a joining device. Compound sentences so punctuated—as in sentence 2—are called *comma splices* (see section 13). As indicated in section 35, if a compound sentence is joined by one of the coordinating conjunctions, a comma should be put in front of the conjunction to mark off the end of one independent clause from the beginning of the next independent clause. But whenever a coordinating conjunction is not present to join the independent clauses, a semicolon must be used to join them. The semicolon serves both to mark the division between the two clauses and to join them.

41

In sentence 5, the semicolon has been used to join two units of unequal rank. That is, there is an independent clause on the left-hand side of the semicolon but not on the right-hand side. To revise this sentence, we converted the string of words on the right-hand side of the semicolon into an independent clause: **these irregular surges prove that the safety devices designed for this project have not yet been perfected.** In the revised sentence, then, the semicolon separates two units of equal rank; that is, two independent clauses.

Sometimes it is advisable to use both a semicolon and a coordinating conjunction to join the independent clauses of a compound sentence. When the clauses are unusually long and have commas within them, a semicolon placed before the coordinating conjunction helps to signal the end of one clause and the beginning of the next one, as in this example:

> Struggling to salvage what was left of the project, he pleaded with his supervisor, who was notoriously softhearted, to grant him an extension of time to complete his investigation, to draw his conclusions, and to make his report; but he forgot that, even with the best of intentions, he had only so many hours a day in which he could work productively.

Here the coordinating conjunction **but** serves to join the two main clauses of the compound sentence, but the use of the semicolon in addition to the conjunction makes it easier for us to read the sentence.

42 Colon to Complete a Lead-in Sentence

Use a colon after a grammatically complete lead-in sentence that formally announces a subsequent numbering, specification, illustration, or extended quotation.

42

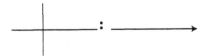

A colon signals that what follows it is a spelling out, a detailing of what was formally announced in the clause on the left-hand side of the colon. What differentiates the colon from the dash as a symbolic mark of punctuation is that the colon throws the reader's attention *forward*, whereas the dash, as a linking device, throws the reader's attention *backward* (see section 43 for further explanation). Although a word, phrase, clause, or series of words, phrases, or clauses can follow the colon, there must be an independent clause (a grammatically complete sentence) on the left-hand side of the colon. The words to the right of the colon complete the sentence.

Conventional Uses for Colons

1. Within a sentence before a list of items, an appositive, or a short quotation:

   Colon before list:

   > CFCs are a family of chemicals that contain three common elements in varying quantities: chlorine, fluorine, and carbon.

Colon before appositive:

UV-B, a particular band of ultraviolet radiation, has terrifying effects on the very building block of life: DNA.

Colon before a short quotation:

Scientists have informed Congress: "The steady increase in skin cancer of recent years is caused not by more sunbathing but by a thinning of the ozone."

42

2. After a lead-in sentence that introduces an extended quotation:

Professor Yoko Tomida has testified that the blips on the monitor do not necessarily indicate lunar emanations:
Many astronomers have labored under the false impression that the magnetic fields that have been recorded on their oscilloscopes represent emanations from the surface of the moon. But a series of recent experiments has conclusively discredited that traditional view. The current opinion is that these electronic blips on our screens were produced by electrical pulsations from black holes in that part of the galaxy. The findings of my studies support this opinion.

Sample revisions:

Original (1): The survey revealed that the four most common terms for the practice of searching for a Saturday-night date are: *scope, scam, pick up,* and *cruise.* **(enumeration)**

Revision: The survey revealed that the four most common terms for the practice of searching for a Saturday-night date are these: *scope, scam, pick up,* and *cruise.*

Original (2): There are two distinct advantages to using physical and/or cultural control methods rather than insecticidal chemicals to reduce insect activity, (1) no chemical residue remains on crops and plants, and (2) no selection to resistance occurs in subsequent generations. **(specification)**

Revision: There are two distinct advantages to using physical and/or cultural control methods rather than insecticidal chemicals to reduce insect activity: (1) no chemical residue remains on crops and plants, and (2) no selection to resistance occurs in subsequent generations.

42

Original (3): The reason given for the failure of the system was incontrovertible—the electrical-supply source was defective. **(explanation)**

Revision: The reason given for the failure of the system was incontrovertible: the electrical-supply source was defective.

Original (4): Michael Jordan employed this strategy for helping his colleagues to settle their contracts and return to the team. After indicating early that he would clearly prefer not to play without the support of his colleagues, he maintained his silence while the negotiating parties worked through their differences. **(illustration)**

Revision: Michael Jordan employed this strategy for helping his colleagues to settle their contracts and return to the team: after indicating early that he would clearly prefer not to play without the support of his colleagues, he maintained his silence while the negotiating parties worked through their differences.

Original (5): With thirty days' notice, all terms of the agreement are subject to: amendment, modification, or termination. **(appositive)**

Revision: With thirty days' notice, all terms of the agreement are subject to three types of alteration: amendment, modification, or termination.

Original (6): Jerome Bruner explains that language use is built on a scaffold of practical experiences which is when "Children learn to use language initially to get what they want, to play games, to stay connected with those on whom they are dependent." **(quotation)**

Revision: Jerome Bruner explains that language use is built on a scaffold of practical experiences: "Children learn to use language initially to get what they want, to play games, to stay connected with those on whom they are dependent."

42

Explanation:

Punctuating sentence 1 as it is originally is like punctuating the following sentence this way:

My name is: John Adams.

In both cases, the words following the colon are needed to complete the sentence grammatically. So either the colon must be dropped altogether, or enough words must be added to make the clause on the left-hand side of the colon a complete sentence. We revised sentence 1 by adding **these,** but you might also use the words **as follows** after the verb **are.**

In sentence 2, the comma after **reduce insect activity** should be replaced with a colon. Since the lead-in clause in sentence 3 throws the reader's attention *forward* to get the reason for the failure, the dash after **incontrovertible** should be replaced by a colon. In sentence 4, we should link the second sentence to the first sentence by substituting a colon for the period after the word **team.** We could revise sentence 5 simply by deleting the colon after the word **to.** However, we have chosen to complete the sentence before the colon with an noun phrase.

In sentence 6, we use a colon to separate the independent clause introducing the quotation from the complete sentence that is quoted.

43 Dash Before Summations

Use a dash when the word or word group that follows it constitutes a summation, a reversal, a commentary, or an amplification of what went before it.

—

Unlike the colon (see section 42), which directs the reader's attention *forward,* the dash usually directs the reader's attention *backward.* What follows the dash, when it is used as a linking device, looks back to what preceded it for the particulars or the details that spell out the meaning or invest the meaning with pungency or irony.

The colon and the dash are usually not interchangeable marks of punctuation. They signal a different relationship between the word groups that precede them and those that follow them. After much practice in reading and writing, one develops a sense of the subtle distinction in relationships signaled by the punctuation in the following sentences.

43

Distinguishing Use of Dash from Use of Colon

IF: The reader's attention is directed *backward:*

The people clearly indicated their indifference to the provocative speech an apathy that later came back to haunt them.

THEN: Use a dash (see p. 131 for correct formation of dash).

The people clearly indicated their indifference to the provocative speech—an apathy that later came back to haunt them.

IF: The reader's attention is directed *forward:*

The reaction of the crowd signified only one thing apathy.

THEN: Use a colon.

The reaction of the crowd signified only one thing: apathy.

Explanation:

In the first sentence in the box above, the lead-in sentence before the colon clearly alerts the reader to expect a specification of what is hinted at in that sentence. In the second sentence, there is no such alerting of the reader, but following the dash, there is an unexpected commentary that forces the reader to look backward and that receives special emphasis by being set off with a dash. The colon and the dash are both linking devices, but they signal different kinds of thought relationships between the parts of the sentence. Frequently, the dash signals a less formal relationship than the colon does.

43

Sample revisions:

Original (1): Statistics 502, Mathematics 421, Computer Graphics 542, and Economics 448, these are the courses that I regard as being pertinent to the job for which I am applying.

Revision: Statistics 502, Mathematics 421, Computer Graphics 542, and Economics 448—these are the courses that I regard as being pertinent to the job for which I am applying. **(summation)**

Original (2): If he was criticized, he would become sullen and tight-lipped, a reaction that did not endear him to his colleagues.

Revision: If he was criticized, he would become sullen and tight-lipped—a reaction that did not endear him to his colleagues. **(commentary)**

Original (3): The basic material is constructed of composite synthetics, a graphite fabric wrapped around a hollow rod made of nylon.

Revision: The basic material is constructed of composite synthetics—a graphite fabric wrapped around a hollow rod made of nylon. **(amplification)**

Original (4): Whenever she is corrected in public, she nods in agreement, apologizes for her behavior, thanks the person who corrected her, and then continues to act as she had been acting.

Revision: Whenever she is corrected in public, she nods in agreement, apologizes for her behavior, thanks the person who corrected her—and then continues to act as she had been acting. **(reversal)**

Formation of Dash

44

A dash is made on the word processor or typewriter with *two unspaced* hyphens and with *no space* before the dash or after the dash. (In handwriting, the dash is made slightly longer than a hyphen.)

Correct formation of the dash:

She forgot—if she ever knew—the proper way to form a dash.

---

44 Enclose Parenthetical Elements with Dashes, Parentheses, or Commas

Use a pair of dashes, parentheses, or commas to enclose parenthetical elements that abruptly arrest the normal flow of the sentence to make a qualifying or rectifying comment.

— . . . —

Whether to enclose a parenthetical element with dashes, parentheses, or commas is often a matter more of stylistic strategy than of grammatical necessity. But conventionally, writers mark the highest degree of interruption with dashes, a middle degree with parentheses, and the lowest degree with commas.

44

Deciding When to Use Dashes, Parentheses, or Commas

Degree of interruption	Punctuation to use	When to use
Most emphasis	Dash—	If the elements interrupt emphasis or shift the normal syntactical flow of the sentence, use a pair of dashes: In some instance—although no one will admit it—the police over-reacted to the provocation.
Moderate emphasis	Parentheses (. . .)	If the parenthetical element mainly adds information or identification, use a pair of parentheses: All the companies that used the service were charged a small fee (usually $500) and were required to sign a contract (an "exclusive-use agreement"). (*$500* names the fee, and *exclusive-use agreement* names the type of contract.)
Least emphasis	Commas , . . . ,	If the parenthetical element mildly interrupts the sentence, use a pair of commas: Albert Einstein, most agree, is the premiere figure of modern physics.

Sample revisions:

Original (1): I learned from this situation, and so will you, that if something sounds totally illogical to you, it probably is.

Revision: I learned from this situation—and so will you—that if something sounds totally illogical to you, it probably is.

Original (2): One of them (let me call him Jim Prude) is clean-shaven and dresses like an Ivy Leaguer of the late 1950s.

Revision: One of them—let me call him Jim Prude—is clean-shaven and dresses like an Ivy Leaguer of the late 1950s.

Original (3): The research team faced the difficulty, or should I say the impossibility, of controlling the temperatures to which the shrubs were exposed.

Revision: The research team faced the difficulty—or should I say the impossibility—of controlling the temperatures to which the shrubs were exposed.

45

With practice, writers develop an ear for the differences in degree of interruption and emphasis and consequently learn to make effective choices among these punctuation marks.

45 Quotation Marks with Period and Comma

The period or the comma always goes inside the closing quotation marks.

." ,"

The American convention for the placement of the period and the comma in relation to the closing quotation mark is almost universally to put the period or comma *inside* the closing quotation mark. The advantage of such consistency is that you never have to pause and ask yourself, "Is this a case where the period goes *inside* or *outside* the quotation mark?" Whether the quotation is a single word or a phrase or a dependent clause or an independent clause, the period or comma always goes *inside* the closing quotation mark.

🖙 Note

In the case of a quotation within a quotation, both the single-stroke quotation mark and the double-stroke quotation mark go *outside* the period or comma, as in this example:

"I read recently," he said, "that Patrick Henry never said, 'Give me liberty or give me death.' "

45

Sample revisions:

Original (1): Anxious to find out my class schedule for the autumn quarter, I ripped open the envelope and discovered the chilling notation "Closed out".

Revision: Anxious to find out my class schedule for the autumn quarter, I ripped open the envelope and discovered the chilling notation "Closed out."

Original (2): "Research papers are still viewed", one student said," as only an assignment and not a learning experience."

Revision: "Research papers are still viewed," one student said, "as only an assignment and not a learning experience."

Original (3): In his *Philosophical Grammar,* Noah Webster paid homage to national usage by accepting *you was* because "national usage determines correctness in grammar".

Revision: In his *Philosophical Grammar,* Noah Webster paid homage to national usage by accepting *you was* because "national usage determines correctness in grammar."

Original (4): "Most teachers give research papers out of habit or tradition", one student commented.

Revision: "Most teachers give research papers out of habit or tradition," one student commented.

Original (5): "Of course "! she exclaimed. "I always gave them what I thought they wanted to read, not what I cared to write".

Revision: "Of course!" she exclaimed. "I always gave them what I thought they wanted to read, not what I cared to write."

46 Quotation Marks with Colon and Semicolon

46

The colon or semicolon always goes outside the closing quotation mark.

$$"; \quad ";$$

Whereas the period or comma always goes *inside* the closing quotation mark, the colon or the semicolon always goes *outside* it. Whenever writers have occasion to use quotation marks with a colon or a semicolon, they have only to recall that the convention governing the placement of the colon or the semicolon in relation to the closing quotation marks is just the *opposite* of the convention for the placement of the period and the comma.

Sample revisions:

Original (1): The participants in the seminar considered the following sequence of activities a "normal load:" working, eating, exercising, studying, and sleeping.

Revision: The participants in the seminar considered the following sequence of activities a "normal load": working, eating, exercising, studying, and sleeping.

Original (2): There is an old, common proverb that says, "The family that prays together stays together;" yet unfortunately, that is not always as true as we would like to believe.

Revision: There is an old, common proverb that says, "The family that prays together stays together⬤ yet unfortunately, that is not always as true as we would like to believe.

Original (3): "The family that prays together and plays together will more often stay together⬤" that is the lesson my family learned from Willow on Wheels (WOW).

47

Revision: The family that prays together and plays together will more often stay together⬤ that is the lesson my family learned from Willow on Wheels (WOW).

47 Quotation Marks with the Question Mark

The question mark sometimes goes inside, sometimes outside, the closing quotation mark.

?"   "?

Although a period or comma always goes inside the closing quotation mark and a colon or semicolon always goes outside the closing quotation mark, you have to consider the individual case before deciding whether to put the question mark inside or outside the closing quotation mark. Fortunately, the criteria for determining whether the question mark goes inside or outside the quotation mark are fairly simple to apply.

Deciding Whether to Put Question Marks Inside or Outside Quotation Marks

Question mark outside:
When the whole sentence but not the unit enclosed in quotation marks is a question, the question mark goes outside the closing quotation mark.

Example A: What official said, "You will not manipulate your statistics to make them say what you want them to say"?

Question mark inside:

When only the unit enclosed in quotation marks is a question, the question mark goes inside the closing quotation mark.

Example B: The students asked the physicist, "What makes it spin?"

Question mark inside:

When the whole sentence and the unit enclosed in quotation marks are both questions, the question mark goes inside the closing quotation mark.

Example C: When will they stop asking, "Is O.J. really responsible for the death of Nicole Brown Simpson?"

47

☞ Note

Whenever the question mark occurs at the end of a sentence, it serves as the terminal punctuation for the entire sentence. In example B, for instance, you do not add a period outside the closing quotation mark, and in example C, you do not need to add another question mark outside the closing quotation mark.

Sample revisions:

Original (1): For a long time, I have wondered, "How do people get drawn into cults"?

Revision: For a long time, I have wondered, "How do people get drawn into cults?"

Original (2): Who once said, "The truth shall set you free?"

Revision: Who once said, "The truth shall set you free"?

Original (3): When do you think this facilitator will finally ask, "What is it about this situation that makes dialogue difficult"?

Revision: When do you think this facilitator will finally ask, "What is it about this situation that makes dialogue difficult?"

48 Italicizing (Underlining) Titles

The titles of books, newspapers, magazines, professional journals, plays, long poems, films, radio programs, television programs, long musical compositions, music albums, works of visual art, and computer software, as well as the names of ships, planes, trains, and spacecraft, should be italicized or underlined.

Choosing Italics (Underlining) or Quotation Marks in Titles

Italics or Underlining	Quotation Marks
Book titles: *The Joy Luck Club* (or <u>The Joy Luck Club</u>)	Short stories: "Big Bertha"
	Chapters or selections: "What Might Rationality Fail to Do?"
Newspaper titles: *Chicago Tribune* (or <u>Chicago Tribune</u>)	Newspaper articles: "Golden Era for Women: "Atlanta Games a Tribute to 24-Year-Old Equality"
	Newspaper section: "Arts and Entertainment"
Journal titles: *Journal of Experimental Biology*	Journal articles: "Curve Walking in Crayfish"
Magazine titles: *Newsweek*	Magazine articles: "Ripping Up Welfare" (from *Time*)

Italics or Underlining	Quotation Marks
Pamphlets: *Separation Anxiety in Dogs*	
Computer software: *Word Perfect* (or Word Perfect)	
Films: *Sense and Sensibility, Jurassic Park*	
Television programs: *E.R., A&E Biography*	Television episodes: **"The Sins of the Father"** (from *Mystery's Inspector Morse*)
Radio programs: *Car Talk, Weekend Edition*	Radio episodes: **"Sweet Corn"** (from *A Prairie Home Companion*)
Lengthy musical compositions: *The Magic Flute*	
Music albums: Eric Clapton's *From the Cradle*	Individual song titles: **"Blues Before Sunrise"**
Comics: *Calvin and Hobbes*	
Plays: *A Streetcar Named Desire*	
Lengthy poems: *Paradise Lost*	Short poems: **"Stopping by Woods on a Snowy Evening"**
Sculpture: Rodin's *The Thinker*	
Paintings: *Mona Lisa*	
Spacecraft: *Voyager II, Enterprise* (or Enterprise)	
Planes: *Enola Gay*	
Ships: the *U.S.S. Boston*	
Trains: the *Zephyr*	

48

Capitalize initial letters and use roman type (no italics or underlining) for the names and abbreviations of books and divisions of the Bible or other sacred books and culturally significant documents:

Genesis	Lk. (Gospel of	Pentateuch
Epistles to the Romans	Luke)	Koran
King James Version	Acts of the Apostles	Pss. (Psalms)
Talmud	Scriptures	Lotus Sutra
Book of Job	Bhagavad Gita	Constitution
Declaration of	Science and Health	Magna Carta
Independence	John 3:16	

48

☞ Note

How do I decide whether a poem is long enough to have its title underlined? A reliable rule of thumb is this: if the poem was ever published as a separate book or if it could conceivably be published as a separate book, it can be considered long enough to have its title underlined.

☞ Note

How do I treat the title of my own unpublished paper for class? (See section 49.)

Original (1): Of Wolves and Men by Barry Lopez combines science, mythology, and cultural studies in its description of the relationship between humans and wolves.

Revision: *Of Wolves and Men* by Barry Lopez combines science, mythology, and cultural studies in its description of the relationship between humans and wolves.

or

<u>Of Wolves and Men</u> by Barry Lopez combines science, mythology, and cultural studies in its description of the relationship between humans and wolves. **(underline or italicize the title of a book)**

Original (2): I learned of your opening for an electrical engineer through your advertisement in the "Phoenix Gazette."

Revision: I learned of your opening for an electrical engineer through your advertisement in the *Phoenix Gazette*. **(underline or italicize the title of a newspaper)**

48

Original (3): "Degrassi High" and "Beverly Hills 90210" are two television programs dealing with similar themes addressed to an adolescent audience.

Revision: <u>Degrassi High</u> and <u>Beverly Hills 90210</u> are two television programs dealing with similar themes addressed to an adolescent audience. **(underline or italicize the name of a television program)**

Original (4): Often, my father told us stories of his tour of duty on the U.S.S. Boston.

Revision: Often, my father told us stories of his tour of duty on the *U.S.S. Boston*. **(underline or italicize the name of a ship)**

Explanation:

Besides being a convention, the use of italics for titles can also protect meaning in some instances. If, for instance, you write "I don't really like Huckleberry Finn," a reader might be uncertain (unless the context gave a clue) whether you were revealing a dislike for Mark Twain's novel or for the character of that name in that novel. Simply by underlining (italicizing) the proper name, you indicate unambiguously that you disliked the novel, not the character.

49 Titles in Quotation Marks

The titles of articles, essays, short poems, songs, chapters of books, short stories, episodes of radio and television programs, and sections of newspapers should be enclosed in quotation marks. (For quick reference, see section 48.)

49

Titles of your own unpublished papers should be neither italicized (underlined) nor put in quotation marks.

The general rule here is that the title of material that is part of a book or periodical or program should be enclosed in quotation marks.

For the title of a paper or report or a proposal that you write, follow the instructions you are given about the format of the title. If you are not given explicit instructions about the format of the title, do not underline (italicize) or enclose the title of your paper in quotation marks. If your title contains elements that are normally underlined or enclosed in quotation marks, those elements, of course, should be underlined or enclosed in quotation marks. The conventional formats of a title of a paper submitted as a class assignment or for publication are illustrated below.

Formatting Titles of Works Submitted to Instructors or Publishers

Original formatting:

"The Palestinian Uprising Through the Eyes of the American Media"

Redefining Hardware and Software Interests in the Age of Microsoft

DANCING WITH WOLVES: A REVIEW OF THE LITERATURE ON CANIS LUPUS AFTER 1960

Revised formatting:

The Palestinian Uprising Through the Eyes of the American Media **(no quotation marks)**

Redefining *Hardware* and *Software* Interests in the Age of Microsoft **(underlining or italicizing only words used as words)**

Dancing with Wolves: A Review of the Literature on *Canis lupus* after 1960 **(capital letters only at the beginning of appropriate words)**

49

Sample revisions:

Original (1): Sylvia Plath's Lady Lazarus, like most of her work, is highly autobiographical.

Revision: Sylvia Plath's "Lady Lazarus," like most of her work, is highly autobiographical.

Original (2): Contrast Rodriguez's experience, then, with the critique of language learning and learning in one's native language that Ngũgĩ wa Thiong'o makes in Decolonising the Mind, one of the essays in his book *Decolonising the Mind: The Politics of Language in African Literature.*

Revision: Contrast Rodriguez's experience, then, with the critique of language learning and learning in one's native language that Ngũgĩ wa Thiong'o offers in "Decolonising the Mind," one of the essays in his book *Decolonising the Mind: The Politics of Language in African Literature.*

Original (3): *Amazing Grace* may be the favorite religious hymn in Protestant churches in the United States.

Revision: "Amazing Grace" may be the favorite religious hymn in Protestant churches in the United States.

Original (4): I never heard my father laugh as hard as he did the night he heard the sketch Tomato Butt on Garrison Keillor's *A Prairie Home Companion*.

Revision: I never heard my father laugh as hard as he did the night he heard the sketch "Tomato Butt" on Garrison Keillor's *A Prairie Home Companion*.

Original (5): In *Two Kinds*, Amy Tan not only states her personal view of growing up but also gives a cultural view of "growing-up" experiences.

Revision: In "Two Kinds," Amy Tan not only states her personal view of growing up but also gives a cultural view of "growing-up" experiences.

50 Italicizing (Underlining) Words Used as Words

<u>Underline</u> (*italicize*) words referred to as words.

Writers can italicize or underline a word to show that it is being used as a *word*, not as a symbol for a thing or an idea:

The class challenged my account of the origin of integrity. **(concept)**
The class challenged my account of the origin of *integrity*. **(word used as word)**

Underlining the word **integrity** in the second sentence above helps the reader of that sentence to read it as the writer intended it to be read; namely, that it was the word, not the virtue, that was being questioned.

Sample revisions:

Original (1): Many of the people who participated in my survey said later that they did not know what inferred meant, although the statistics do not support that revelation.

Revision: Many of the people who participated in my survey said later that they did not know what *inferred* meant, although the statistics do not support that revelation.

or

Many of the people who participated in my survey said later that they did not know what <u>inferred</u> meant, although the statistics do not support that revelation.

Original (2): The term acid rain seems to suggest that rain naturally is free of acid; in fact, acid is present in all rainwater.

50

Revision: The term *acid rain* seems to suggest that rain naturally is free of acid; in fact, acid is present in all rainwater.

Original (3): The dictionary defines "delirium" as a more-or-less temporary disorder of the mental faculties.

Revision: The dictionary defines *delirium* as a more-or-less temporary disorder of the mental faculties.

Original (4): Because of the emphasis on new worldviews, "subjectivity" and "objectivity" are two terms that researchers discuss at length in many disciplines today.

Revision: Because of the emphasis on new worldviews, *subjectivity* and *objectivity* are two terms that researchers discuss at length in many disciplines today.

☞ Note

An alternative but less common device for marking words used as words is to enclose the words in quotation marks as was done in sentence 3 above. Since both devices, underlining (italics) and quotation marks, are authorized by convention, you should adopt one system and use it consistently. The use of underlining (italics) is probably the safer of the two systems, however, because quotation marks are also used to enclose quoted definitions of a word and to enclose quoted words or phrases in the sentence, as in the sentence

We heard her say "yes."

Here, **yes** is not being referred to as a word but is a quotation of what she said.

51 Italicizing (Underlining) Foreign Words

Underline (italicize) foreign words and phrases, unless they have become naturalized or Anglicized.

Writers use underlining (italics) to indicate foreign words and phrases. The graphic device of underlining does not ensure that the reader will be able to translate the foreign expression, but it does prevent confusion by alerting the reader to the presence of non-English words.

Some foreign words and phrases, such as *habeas corpus, divorcée, mania, siesta,* and *subpoena,* have been used so often in an English context that they have been accepted into the vocabulary as "naturalized" or "Anglicized" words and therefore do not need to be italicized. Since dictionaries have a good system of indicating which foreign words and phrases have become naturalized and which have not, you should consult a dictionary when you are in doubt about the current status of a particular foreign word or phrase.

Exception:

Proper nouns designating foreign persons, places, or institutions, even when they retain their native spelling and pronunciation, are *never* italicized.

Pierre Chardin thought that the Bibliothèque Nationale was on the Champs Élysées in Paris.

Sample revisions:

> **Original (1):** It was reasonable for the customer to ask whether our collateral was an adequate "quid pro quo" for the concession that he had made in signing the contract.

> **Revision:** It was reasonable for the customer to ask whether our collateral was an adequate quid pro quo for the concession that he had made in signing the contract.

or

> It was reasonable for the customer to ask whether our collateral was an adequate *quid pro quo* for the concession that he had made in signing the contract.

> **Original (2):** Our French subsidiary considered our questioning of its fiscal responsibility an instance of "lèse-majesté."

> **Revision:** Our French subsidiary considered our questioning of its fiscal responsibility an instance of *lèse-majesté*.

> **Original (3):** There has always been a pronounced revival in Germany of the Weltschmertz that once characterized the mood of the nineteenth-century Romantic poets.

> **Revision:** There has always been a pronounced revival in Germany of the *Weltschmertz* that once characterized the mood of the nineteenth-century Romantic poets.

> **Original (4):** According to the Italians, the rich enjoy "la dolce vita."

> **Revision:** According to the Italians, the rich enjoy *la dolce vita*.

52

52 Hyphens in Compound Words

Compound words should be hyphenated.

English reveals its Germanic origin in its tendency to form compounds; that is, to take two or more words and join them to create a single unit that designates a thing or a concept quite different from what the individual words designate. Dozens of words in English have made this transition from a hyphenated compound to a single amalgamated word (e.g., **basketball, airport, briefcase**). But hundreds of compounds are still printed with a hyphen, either because they have not been used enough to achieve status as unmarked hybrids or because the absence of a hyphen would lead to ambiguity. A reliable dictionary will indicate which compounds have made the passage and which have not.

52

Using Hyphens to Link Compound Words

With the exception of recognized amalgams, a hyphen should be used to link the following:

1. Two or more words functioning as a single grammatical unit:

    She went to visit her **sister-in-law.** (***noun***)
    The gangleader **pistol-whipped** him. (***verb***)
    He conceded the point **willy-nilly.** (***adverb***)

2. Fractions and numbers from (21 to 99) when they are written out:

    one thirty-sixth, one-quarter, twenty-one, forty-eight, ninety-nine

3. Combinations with the prefixes **ex-** and **self-**:

    ex-president, ex-wife, self-denial, self-contradictory

4. Combinations with prefixes like **anti-, pro-, pre-,** and **post-,** when the second element in the combination begins with a capital letter or a number:

    anti-Establishment, pro-American, pre–1960, post–1985

5. Combinations where the unhyphenated compound might be mistaken for another word:

re-cover (the chair)	**recover** (the lost wallet)
re-sign (the contract)	**resign** (the office)
co-op (a cooperative apartment)	**coop** (a pen for chickens)

☞ **Note**

52

With the exceptions noted in 4, compounds formed with prefixes now tend to be written as a single word (for example, *antiknock, nonrestrictive, preconscious, subdivision, postgraduate*).

Sample revisions:

Original (1): Thirty five minutes later, they announced that all air traffic at Midway would remain grounded until the O'Hare traffic had cleared.

Revision: Thirty-five minutes later, they announced that all air traffic at Midway would remain grounded until the O'Hare traffic had cleared.

Original (2): They scheduled the examination in three quarter hour segments.

Revision: They scheduled the examination in three quarter-hour segments.

Original (3): The in flight service, however, was inexcusably poor.

Revision: The in-flight service, however, was inexcusably poor.

Original (4): They were impressed with her never say die attitude.

Revision: They were impressed with her never-say-die attitude.

Original (5): The announcement of another one or two hour delay came as no surprise because the weather was unsuitable for flying.

Revision: The announcement of another one- or two-hour delay came as no surprise because the weather was unsuitable for flying.

Explanation:

Frequently in writing, only a hyphen will clarify ambiguous syntax. In sentence 2, for instance, a reader would have difficulty determining whether the examination was divided into three segments of fifteen minutes each (a meaning that is clearly signaled by this placement of the hyphen: **three quarter-hour segments**) or whether it was divided into segments of forty-five minutes' duration (a meaning that is clearly signaled by this placement of the hyphen: **three-quarter-hour segments**).

Sentence 5 shows how to hyphenate a compound word when there is more than one term on the left side of the hyphenation (**one, two**). In this way, **hour** need not be repeated (as in a **one-hour or two-hour delay**). In typing, insert a space after the hyphen if the hyphen is not immediately followed by the word it is meant to join (**one- or two-hour delay,** *not* **one-or two-hour delay**).

53 Hyphen to Divide Words

A word can be broken and hyphenated at the end of a line only at a syllable break; a one-syllable word should never be broken and hyphenated.

For the writer, two valuable bits of information are supplied by the initial entry of every word in the dictionary: (1) the spelling of a word and (2) the syllabication of the word. Words of more than two syllables can be broken and hyphenated at more than one place. The word *belligerent*, for instance, is entered this way in the dictionary:

bel·lig·er·ent. If that word occurred at the end of a line and you saw that you could not get the whole word in the remaining space, you could break the word and hyphenate it at any of the syllables marked with a raised period.

"Tricks" of Syllabication

53

A word can usually be broken as follows:

1. After a prefix (*con-, ad-, un-, im-*)

   ad-verse   con-fuse

2. Before a suffix (*-tion, -ment, -less, -ous, -ing*)

   ac-tion   fer-ment   care-less

3. Between double consonants

   oc-cur-rence   cop-per   stop-ping

Original: bell-igerent   **Revision:** bel-ligerent

Original: part-icular   **Revision:** par-ticular

Original: stopp-ing   **Revision:** stop-ping

Original: Eng-lish   **Revision:** En-glish

Original: wrench-ed   **Revision:** wrenched

☞ Note

One-syllable words should never be divided and hyphenated no matter how long they are. If you come to the end of a line and find that you do not have enough space for words like **horde, grieve, quaint, wrenched,** or **strength,** leave the space blank, and write the whole word on the next line.

54 Numbers

Observe the conventions governing the use of numbers in written copy.

Conventions for the use of numbers in written copy:

1. Do not begin a sentence with an Arabic numeral; spell out the number or recast the sentence:

   Original: 612 applicants showed up on the first day.

   Revision: Six hundred and twelve applicants showed up on the first day.

2. Spell out any number of fewer than three digits (or any number under 100) when the number is used as an adjective modifying a noun:

   Original: When I was only **5** years old, I could ride a horse.

   Revision: When I was only **five** years old, I could ride a horse.

   Original: Each of the **50** states is entitled to this subsidy.

   Revision: Each of the **fifty** states is entitled to this subsidy.

3. Always use Arabic numerals with **a.m.** and **p.m.** and do not add the redundant **o'clock** and **morning** or **afternoon**:

   Original: The auction started at **four p.m. in the afternoon.**

   Revision: The auction started at **4:00 p.m.**

   or

   The auction started at **four o'clock in the afternoon.**

4. Use Arabic numerals for dates and page numbers:

   Original: I was born on **May twenty-fourth nineteen fifty-four.**

Revision: I was born on **May 24, 1954.**

5. Use Arabic numerals for addresses, dollars and cents, decimals, degrees, measurements (especially when abbreviations are used), and percentages:

> Addresses: 618 N. 29th St.
> Dollars and cents: $4.68, $.15 or 15 cents
> Decimals: 3.14, 0.475
> Degrees: 52°F, 26°C
> Measurements: 3" × 5", 3.75 mi., 2 ft. 9 in., 6' 2" tall (*but* six feet tall)
> Percentages: 6% or 6 percent (always use *percent* with fractional percentages: 6½ percent or 6.5 percent)

Original: The shelf was **six feet four inches** long.

Revision: The shelf was **6 ft. 4 in.** long.

Original: About **six %** of the stores were selling a gross of **three-by-five** index cards for more than **fifty-six dollars and thirty cents.**

Revision: About **6%** of the stores were selling a gross of **3" × 5"** index cards for more than **$56.30.**

55 Capitalization

Observe the conventions governing the capitalization of certain words.

In general, the convention governing capitalization is that the first letter of the proper name (that is, the particular or exclusive name) of persons, places, things, institutions, agencies, nations, and such should be capitalized. While the tendency today is to use lowercase letters for many words that were formerly written or printed with capital letters (for instance, *biblical reference* instead of *Biblical reference*), the use of capital letters still prevails in the written medium in the following cases:

55

1. The first letter of the first word in a sentence:

   They were uncertain about which words should be capitalized.

2. The first letter of the first word of every line of traditional English verse:

   Little fly,
   Thy summer's play
   My thoughtless hand
   Has brushed away.

3. All nouns, pronouns, verbs, adjectives, adverbs, and the first and last words of titles of publications and other artistic works:

   Going to Meet the Man
   "The Place of the Enthymeme in Rhetorical Theory"

4. The first name, middle name or initial, and last name of a person, real or fictional:

T. S. Eliot	Sylvia Marie Mikkelsen
David Letterman	Achilles
Mickey Mouse	Steven M. Finkle

5. The names and abbreviation of villages, towns, cities, counties, states, nations, and regions:

Columbus, Ohio	Cook County	U.S.A.
Canada	South America	the South (but:
Indochina	Arctic Circle	"We drove south")

6. The names of rivers, lakes, falls, oceans, mountains, deserts, and parks:

the Mississippi River	Atlantic
the Grand Tetons	Yellowstone National Park

Lake Erie   Victoria Falls
the Kalahari Desert

7. The names and abbreviations of businesses, industries, institutions, agencies, schools, political parties, religious denominations, and philosophical, scientific, literary, and artistic movements:

The Ohio State University   Democrats
the Republican convention   **C.I.A.**
Communist   Smithsonian Institution
    (but: communist ideology)   Buddhism
Presbyterian   Thomistic philosophy
America West Airlines   Dow Chemical Corporation
the Pentagon   the Nuclear Age
Victorian literature
Addison Wesley Longman Publishers

8. The titles of historical events, epochs, and periods:

Renaissance   Thirty Years' War
World War II   Ice Age
the Middle Ages   the Battle of Gettysburg
Reformation   the Depression

9. Honorary and official titles when they precede the name of a person:

Rabbi Balfour Brickner   Cardinal Joseph Bernardin
the Duke of Cornwall   General Patton
Pope John Paul II   Reverend Billy Graham
Chief Justice Stone   Queen Elizabeth
His (Her) Excellency

10. The names of weekdays, months, holidays, holy days, and other special days or periods:

Christmas Eve   Memorial Day   the first Sunday in June
Passover   the Fourth of July Lent
Mardis Gras   National Book Week

11. The names and abbreviations of the books and divisions of the Bible and other sacred books (no italics for these titles):

Genesis	Pentateuch
Lk. (Gospel of Luke)	Acts of the Apostles
Epistles to the Romans	Koran
King James Version	Scriptures
Talmud	Bhagavad Gita
Book of Job	Lotus Sutra
Pss. (Psalms)	Science and Health

55

Exceptions:

Do not capitalize words like the underlined in the following examples:

the African <u>coast</u>	the river Elbe
(but: the West Coast)	(but: the Elbe River)
<u>northern</u> Wisconsin	the <u>federal government</u>
the <u>senator</u> from Arizona	the <u>presidential itinerary</u>
the <u>municipal library</u>	the <u>county courthouse</u>
in the <u>autumn</u>	they headed <u>west</u>

Sample revisions:

Original (1): The title of the article in *Scientific American* was **"Recent developments in rocket-propulsion fuels."**

Revision: The title of the article in *Scientific American* was "Recent Developments in Rocket-Propulsion Fuels."

Original (2): Dr. Truong Lehang, a renowned professor in the **department of marine biology** at this Canadian university, has been studying the migratory habits of whales in **the arctic, the northeast,** and **the pacific northwest.**

Revision: Dr. Truong Lehang, a renowned professor in the Department of Marine Biology at this Canadian university, has been studying the migratory habits of whales in the Arctic, the Northeast, and the Pacific Northwest.

Original (3): The prime vacation time for most Americans is the period between **the fourth of july** and **labor day.**

Revision: The prime vacation time for most Americans is the period between the Fourth of July and Labor Day.

55

Research Writing and Documentation

A research paper reports the results of some investigation, experiment, interview, or reading that you have done. Some of the ordinary papers you write are also based on personal investigations, interviews, and reading, and when your paper is based on data derived from research, you should acknowledge the source of the data. For instance, you can reveal the source of information or quotations by saying, right in the text of the paper, "Mr. Stanley Smith, the director of the Upward Bound project, with whom I talked last week, confirmed the rumor that . . ." or "James Reston said in his column in last Sunday's *New York Times* that . . ." Authors of research papers also use identifying lead-ins like those, but in addition, they supply—usually in parenthetical references—any further information (such as the exact date of the newspaper they are quoting from and the number of the page from which the quotation was taken) that readers would need if they wanted to check the sources. By revealing this specific information about the source, authors enable readers to check the accuracy and fairness of the reporting, and they enhance their own credibility with their readers.

In the pages that follow, we will present some advice about gathering and reporting material from outside sources, some models of parenthetical forms of documentation, some models of the bibliography listed at the end of a paper, and some samples of typescript pages from research papers. The instructor or the publication that you write for may prescribe a format that differs from the directions given here, but if no specific instructions are given, you can follow these suggestions and models with the assurance that they conform to the prevailing conventions for research papers written in most fields. The format for documenting references, citations, and quotations may differ slightly from discipline to discipline, but whether you are writing a research paper in the humanities or in one of the physical or social sciences, the same kind of basic information about the sources is supplied in the documentation.

56

56 Selecting an Appropriate Subject

Taking special care in selecting an appropriate subject for your research paper will, in the long run, make the task of writing the paper easier and increase your chances of getting a good grade for your efforts. Sometimes, you will have a completely free choice of a subject for your paper; at other times, your instructor will set up a list of subjects or a general category of subjects from which you may choose. In either case, the ultimate choice of a specific subject will be yours. Make this choice conscientiously and judiciously.

A number of considerations will guide you in selecting an appropriate subject: (1) the physical limits set for the paper, in terms of either the number of words (e.g., 2,500–3,000 words) or the number of pages (e.g., eight to ten pages); (2) the time available to you, from the initial assignment to the final due date; (3) your particular interests; (4) the research facilities available to you; (5) the defined limits of the subject; and (6) a determination of the main point you want to make about the subject you have chosen.

Suppose that from a list of topics suggested by your instructor, you chose this one: The Use of Computers in the Schools. You chose that subject partly because it interests you (point 3 above) and partly because you are sure that your school library has lots of material on this timely subject (point 4). Because you have only five weeks in which to do the research and write the paper (point 2), and because the instructor set a limit of 2,000–2,500 words (eight to ten double-spaced pages at 250 words per page) for the paper (point 1), you realize that you must narrow the broad subject that you have chosen (point 5) and must determine the main point you want to make about the subject that you finally select (point 6).

56   By chipping away at your broad subject, you can get it down to manageable proportions. You decide that you do not want to consider *all* the possible uses of computers in the schools, so you confine yourself to just the use of word processors. *Schools* is too broad a category for this paper, so you decide to concentrate on the undergraduate college scene. You further narrow the subject by specifying the use of the word processor in the college-freshman composition classroom. Now that you have a sharply defined subject (point 5) that can be managed within the limits set for you (points 1, 2, 3, and 4), you must decide what point you want to make about that subject (point 6). After careful deliberation, you settle on a focus and decide to formulate that focus in a statement of purpose rather than in a thesis sentence: you want to investigate some of the successes that colleges in the United States have had in improving the writing of students by using word processors in first-year composition courses.

Now you are ready to do the research necessary to write a paper on the subject that you have carefully selected and narrowed. After some careful deliberations, you decide that your research for this project will consist primarily of finding and reading articles in professional journals that deal with the use of word processors in first-year writing courses, of visiting your campus writing classes that use word processors, and of talking with the students and instructors in those classes. You will be using the resources of the school library, visiting the composition classrooms where word processors are used, and interviewing students and teachers in those writing laboratories.

57 Using the Library

You have determined that your research will involve you, at least partly, in the reading of books and articles. The main source of books and articles is the library—either the public library or your school's library. Perhaps the chief benefit that you derive from doing a research paper is that this exercise forces you to become acquainted with the library and its resources. Becoming aware of the wealth of knowledge stored in the library and getting to know *where* the various sources of wealth are and *how* to use them will be a valuable part of your general education.

The best way to get acquainted with the library is to visit it, to look around, to examine the card catalog or the electronic indexes to the resources of the library, to take some books down from the shelves and open them, and, above all, to use the library. But if you want to speed up the getting-acquainted process, you can consult a book like Eugene P. Sheehy's *A Guide to Reference Books* (10th ed. Chicago: American Library Association of Chicago, 1986). Another helpful guide, widely used in the colleges and universities, is James D. Lester's *Writing Research Papers: A Complete Guide* (8th ed. New York: HarperCollins, 1996). The second chapter of this book is devoted to helpful information about the resources of the library, including a section on "The Electronic Library: Using a Computer Search." Consulting books like these in conjunction with your visits to the library will prepare you to do research in printed sources for most of your classes.

Remember that for your research on the use of the word processor, you determined that in addition to doing research in the library, you were going to visit some of the composition classrooms where word processors are being used and to interview students and teachers in those writing laboratories. For all three of these kinds of research, you will have to develop some system of taking notes. What follows may help you develop that system.

Taking notes

If you do enough research, you will eventually develop the system of gathering notes that works best for you. Some people, for instance, just scribble their notes on full sheets of paper or in spiral notebooks. Others record their notes and quotations on 3"×5" or 4"×6" cards—*one* note or quotation to a card. The advantage of recording notes on separate cards is that you can later select and arrange the cards to suit the order in which you are going to use them in your paper. It is considerably more difficult to select and arrange notes if they are written out, one after the other, on full sheets of paper. You could, of course, cut out notes from the full sheets, but that activity involves an extra step.

57

Each note card should be self-contained: that is, it should contain all the information you would need to document that material properly if you used it in your paper. A note card is self-contained if you never have to go back to the original source to recover any bit of information about the note. So each note card should include the following:

1. The particular information you wish to record.
2. Your own shorthand system of referring to the source of the information—for example, the author's last name or a short version of the title—and the page(s) on which the information appeared in the original source.
3. An indication of whether the note is a summary, a paraphrase, or a direct quotation.

Accuracy in notes

Whenever you are transmitting information that you have appropriated from others, you must be scrupulously careful about the accuracy of that information. The question of accuracy is complicated by considerations of whether the material you are transmitting represents a *summary* or a *paraphrase* or a *direct quotation*. If you are transmitting the material in the form of a direct quotation, that quotation must be reproduced exactly as it appeared in the original source. You must not inadvertently add or omit or misspell any words. If you deliberately add words to a direct quotation, you must put those words in square brackets:

```
The president said, "He [William Bennett] sig-
nificantly changed the direction in which NEH
[National Endowment for the Humanities] was
headed that year [1985]."
```

57

If you deliberately omit words from a direct quotation, you must use ellipsis periods to signal that omission:

```
The authors of the report say, "Blending may
seem simple to an adult who already knows how
to read, but . . . it is a difficult step for
many children."
```

If a word was misspelled in the original source, you must reproduce that misspelling in the quotation and signal that the misspelling is not yours by inserting *sic* ("thus") in square brackets:

```
"That is the most flattering complement [sic] I
have ever received," Professor James said in a
letter to the editor.
```

Accuracy is a more relative matter when you transmit appropriated information in the form of a paraphrase or a summary. What paraphrase and summary have in common is that they represent an attempt to render in one's own words information gathered from some outside source. The difference between a paraphrase and a summary is that a paraphrase tends to be a translation of something said in a few sentences, whereas a summary tends to be a translation of something said over several paragraphs or pages. We can objectively judge the accuracy of a direct quotation by checking to see whether the quotation is an exact transcription of the original words, but our judgment about the accuracy of a paraphrase or a summary is bound to be more subjective and therefore relative.

Here is a direct quotation from Thomas Babington Macaulay's essay-review of Leopold von Ranke's classic *Ecclesiastical and Political History of the Popes of Rome During the Sixteenth and Seventeenth Centuries* (1840) and five attempts to paraphrase a part of, or to summarize the whole of, this passage:

57

> During the eighteenth century, the influence of the Church of Rome was constantly on the decline. Unbelief made extensive conquests in all the Catholic countries of Europe and in some countries obtained a complete ascendancy. The Papacy was at length brought so low as to be an object of derision to infidels and of pity rather than of hatred to Protestants. During the nineteenth century, this fallen Church has been gradually rising from her depressed state and reconquering her old dominion. No person who calmly reflects on what, within the last few years, has passed in Spain, in Italy, in South America, in Ireland, in the Netherlands, in Prussia, even in France, can doubt that the power of this Church over the hearts and minds of men is now far greater than it was when the Encyclopaedia and the Philosophical Dictionary appeared.

1. Macaulay maintains that the influence of the Catholic Church was greater in the nineteenth century than at any other time in its history.

2. During the 1700s, according to Thomas B. Macaulay, the influence of the Catholic Church was constantly on the decline.

3. The Roman papacy, Macaulay avers, is despised by infidels and hated by Protestants.

4. During the eighteenth century, skepticism, Macaulay says, increased in all the Catholic countries of Europe.

5. Thomas Babington Macaulay's thesis is that although the influence of the Roman Catholic Church declined during the eighteenth century, that Church regained its power in Europe during the nineteenth century.

57

Sentence 1 is an inaccurate paraphrase of the last sentence of the quotation from Macaulay, for what Macaulay said in that final sentence is that the influence of the Catholic Church was greater now in the nineteenth century than it had been in the eighteenth century, when the *Encyclopaedia* and the *Philosophical Dictionary* were published.

Sentence 2 is a fairly accurate paraphrase of the first sentence of the original, but the wording and the structure of that paraphrase are so close to the original that this sentence could be regarded as an instance of plagiarism.

Sentence 3 is a slightly inaccurate paraphrase of Macaulay's third sentence, because in relation to that sentence, it states a half-truth: the papacy was derided by infidels but, according to Macaulay, only during the eighteenth century, and while the papacy may have been hated by Protestants at an earlier time, it was pitied rather than hated in the eighteenth century. In short, the paraphrase is misleading.

If the word *skepticism* can be regarded as a synonym for Macaulay's *unbelief,* sentence 4 is an accurate paraphrase of the second sentence of the quotation.

Sentence 5 is an accurate summary of the main point of the quotation from Macaulay.

Note the varying degrees of inaccuracy—or accuracy—that we have observed in the five translations. The inaccuracies are instances of a slight or an egregious misreading of a text, but whether a particular reader would be sharp enough to detect the misreading is uncertain. However, the ideal that all readers and writers should strive for is scrupulous accuracy. Probably none of the inaccurate readings of Macaulay's text would prompt a teacher to give a failing grade to a paper in which any one of those inaccurate readings occurred, but one hopes that a teacher would at least make some kind of remark in the margin of the paper that would question the accuracy of that reading. It is much more important for all of us to become accurate readers and writers than to get a high grade on a paper we write.

58

58 Incorporating Sources

What needs to be documented?

As you draft your paper, you will have to develop a sense of what needs to be documented. Here are some guidelines to help you:

1. Any direct quotation should be followed by a citation of the source. Be sure to enclose the quotation in quotation marks, unless it is a *long* quotation. (See below for how to present a long quotation.)

2. Paraphrased material may or may not need to be followed by a parenthetical citation of the source. If, for instance, the fact or information that you report in your own words is *generally known* by people knowledgeable on the subject, you probably do not have to document that paraphrased material. For example, if you were writing a research paper on the assassination of Abraham Lincoln, you would ordinarily not have to document your statement that John Wilkes Booth shot Lincoln in Ford's Theater in Washington, D.C., in April 1865, because those historical facts are common knowledge. But if one of the arguments in your paper concerned the *exact time of the day* when he was shot, you would have to document your statement that Lincoln was shot at 8:40 p.m. on the evening of April 14,

1865. When, however, you cannot resolve your doubt about whether paraphrased material needs to be documented, document it.

3. When you are summarizing, in your own words, a great deal of information that you have gathered from your reading, you can be spared having to document several sentences in that summary by using a *content endnote*. (See the discussion on p. 178 regarding the proper use and format of endnotes.)

58

Plagiarism

If you present as your own words what you have copied from some other author or if you present some paraphrased material without acknowledging the source of the information, you are guilty of plagiarism. (See the section on "Accuracy in Notes," pp. 162–166, for some examples of acceptable and unacceptable paraphrases.) The academic community regards plagiarism as a very serious offense, punishable by a failing grade on a paper, a failing grade in the course, or dismissal from school. If you value your personal integrity and your status in school, you should resist the temptation to engage in this kind of intellectual dishonesty. For what needs to be documented in a paper, see the three guidelines in the previous section.

Keep quotations to a minimum

A research paper should not be just a pastiche of long quotations stitched together by an occasional comment or by a transitional sentence from the author of the paper. You should use your own words as much as possible, and when you do quote, you should keep the quotations brief. Often, a quoted phrase or sentence will make a point more emphatically than a long quotation. You must learn to look for the phrase or sentence that represents the kernel of the quotation and to use that extract rather than the full quotation. Otherwise, the point you want to make with the quotation may be lost in all the verbiage. You will be more likely to keep your quotations short if you try to work most of them into the framework of your own sentence, like this:

> The New York Times claims that the recent in-
> crease in enrollments at community colleges
> across the nation is "the main reason that
> total enrollment in higher education has not
> fallen, as educational forecasters expected
> would happen by now" (Maeroff).

58

Sometimes, however, when you find it difficult to present the essential point in a short extract, you will have to quote something at greater length. Long quotations (two sentences or more) should be *inset* ten spaces from the left-hand margin, with *no quotation marks enclosing the quotation,* and *triple space* between the long quotation and the rest of the text:

> Statistical studies have been made of
> the most common categories of dreams--
> studies which, at least to some ex-
> tent, ought to illuminate the nature
> of dreams. In a survey of the dreams
> of college students, the following
> were, in order, the five most frequent
> types: (1) falling; (2) being pursued
> or attacked; (3) attempting repeatedly
> and unsuccessfully to perform a task;
> (4) various academic learning experi-
> ences; and (5) diverse sexual experi-
> ences (164-165).

Ellipsis periods

Ellipsis periods (three spaced periods) are used to indicate that a word or several words or whole sentences have been omitted from a direct quotation:

```
The President said last week that "the American
people . . . would not tolerate such violence."
```

(*Note that there should be a space between periods; wrong form:* ...)

58

The three spaced periods indicate that a string of words has been omitted. To indicate the deletion of whole sentences, insert the three ellipsis periods, while retaining any punctuation that preceded the insertion of the three ellipsis periods. (The period after the word *context* below is the usual period that marks the end of a sentence.)

```
These results have no connection with any gen-
uine attempt to use words in a normally ex-
pected context. . . . A similar artificial mon-
strosity could be contrived by jumbling
together inappropriate metaphors.
```

Usually, there is no need to put ellipsis periods at the beginning or end of a quotation, because the reader knows that the quotation has been extracted from a larger context. Reserve ellipsis period for indicating omissions *within* quotations. Take care that such omissions do not destroy the original meaning or intent of the original passage.

Square brackets

Square brackets are used to enclose anything that the author of the research paper inserts into a direct quotation:

```
About this tendency to indulge in scatological
language, H. A. Taine wrote, "He [Swift] drags
```

poetry not only through the mud, but into the
filth; he rolls in it like a raging madman; he
enthrones himself in it and bespatters all
passers-by."

The Senator was emphatic in stating his reaction to the measure: "This action by HEW
[Health, Education, and Welfare] will defi-
nitely not reverse the downward spiral [of
prices and wages] that has plagued us for the
last eight months."

We find this entry in the Japanese admiral's
diary: "Promptly at 8:32 on Sunday morning of
December 6 [sic], 1941, I dispatched the first
wave of bombers for the raid on Perl Harber
[sic]."

If your typewriter does not have keys that make square brackets, you
will have to draw the brackets with a pen after you remove the paper
from the typewriter; leave spaces for the brackets.

59 Evaluating Sources

Probably the last skill you will acquire that is connected with the
writing of a research paper is the ability to review the sources you
have discovered and to make intelligent judgments about their rele-
vance, validity, and rhetorical effectiveness for the research paper you
are going to write. It is the rare freshman student who can make
those intelligent judgments. Maybe by the time a student has had a
few courses in a chosen major, he or she will be able to make fruitful

assessments of the collected sources. But most college-level students do not securely acquire that ability until they are faced with the task of writing a thesis for an M.A. degree or a dissertation for a Ph.D. In short, one does not really acquire this skill until one has had considerable experience in doing serious research and in writing papers based on that research.

But most undergraduate students have to do some research in their lower-level courses and to write a paper based on that research. Of course, their instructors will give them some directions about that research and about the writing of the paper. Almost inevitably, students in a second-semester or third-quarter Freshman English class will be required to write a research paper. What we can do here is give these amateur researchers some tips about how to assess the material they have found and to make intelligent choices of the material most pertinent to the main point of the research paper.

59

1. **Examine the peripheral apparatus of the book or article to get some idea of whether this source is relevant to the research paper you intend to write.** You can examine such parts of the book or article as the dust jacket, the table of contents, the preface or introduction or abstract, the footnotes, the endnotes, the indexes, the bibliographies, and any identification given of the author or authors.

2. **Check the date of publication.** Sometimes a later date may ensure that additional information is given about the subject or that corrections have been made of previous information.

3. **Check the medium in which the book or article was published.** If a book, was it published by a university press or by a commercial press? If an article, was it published in a scholarly journal, such as *Rhetoric Review, Library Journal, Social Education,* or *Journal of Bacteriology*? Or was it published in one of the serious periodicals, such as *Scientific American, The New Yorker,* or *Saturday Review*? Or was it published in one of the popular magazines, such as *Time, Newsweek,* or *Sports Illustrated*?

4. **Can you determine the primary audience for this book or article?** Does the book or article appeal primarily to a conservative audience or to a liberal audience? to a working-class audience or to an executive-class audience? to Christians, Muslims, or Taoists? to Catholics, Protestants, or Jews? to women or men? to pro-choice advocates or to pro-life advocates? Determining the audience may give you a tip-off about the bias of the article. If you can detect the particular bias of the article, can you determine whether that bias has distorted some of the facts, information, or interpretations presented in the article? However, remember that even if you can determine the particular bias of the book or article, the book or article may still be useful for your research paper.

5. **See if you can determine whether the book or article that you are considering is a mixture of primary and secondary sources or whether its sources are predominantly or exclusively primary or secondary.** *Primary* documents are those that other people later comment on or interpret or evaluate—documents such as novels, poems, plays, diaries, memoirs, interviews or reports on experiments, surveys, and scientific studies. These later commentaries, interpretations, or evaluations are called *secondary* documents. The ideal research paper is one that combines primary sources with secondary sources. But a research paper that is exclusively secondary is not necessarily inferior to a combination of primary and secondary sources. You just should be aware of the difference between primary and secondary sources.

If you make use of the five tips given here to assess the various sources that you have discovered in your searches, you will have made a giant step toward writing a research paper that will elicit praise from your instructor and that will give you a feeling of significant achievement.

60 Documentary Systems

This is the point at which to mention three very thorough and helpful books about the preparations for and the writing of a research paper:

1. James D. Lester. *Writing Research Papers: A Complete Guide.* 8th ed. New York: HarperCollins, 1996.
2. Kate L. Turabian. *A Manual for Writers of Term Papers, Theses, and Dissertations.* 6th ed. Chicago: University of Chicago Press, 1996.
3. Joseph Gibaldi. *MLA Handbook for Writers of Research Papers.* 4th ed. New York: Modern Language Association of America, 1995.

60

Any one of these three books will provide beginning writers of research papers with *more* guidance than a little handbook like this one can give. What we will do in this section is present the documentary systems for the humanities (Modern Language Association—MLA), the social sciences (American Psychological Association—APA), the biological sciences (Council of Biology Editors—CBE), as well as the oldest of all the documentary systems (the footnote system, as presented by *The Chicago Manual of Style*) and the newest of the documentary styles, the one for on-line research (Alliance for Computers and Writing—ACW).

Once you have written your research paper, you will have to document your paper. That is, you will have to indicate, by means of a notation system that is standard for papers written in a particular discipline, where you got the quotations, the citations, the facts, the commentaries, and the interpretations you have presented in your paper. We will present here a number of documentary systems, not only for quotations, commentaries, paraphrases, and so on in the text of your paper but also for the bibliography at the end of your paper.

These are the prescribed documentary systems for most of the research that has been published in this country.

61 The MLA System

61

In the second edition of the *MLA Handbook for Writers of Research Papers* (1984) and in the subsequently published *MLA Style Manual* (1985), the Modern Language Association presented its radical change in the style of documenting research papers, a style that had been standard for most books and journals in the humanities since the first edition of the *MLA Style Sheet* appeared in 1951. Instead of indicating the source of quotations and citations in footnotes or in endnotes, the MLA system now uses a parenthetical style of documentation, much like the APA system. The MLA Committee on Research Activities believes that this new system of documentation is characterized by "precision, accuracy, economy, consistency, clarity, and comprehensibility" and that it will help to bridge the gap that had existed between the documentation system in the humanities and that in other disciplines.

The two substantive consequences of the change are (1) that footnotes or endnotes are no longer used to indicate the source of quotations and citations that appear in the text of a research paper and (2) that all researched essays—even those published in professional journals—carry a bibliography of all the works cited in the paper. The essence of the new style of documentation is that some kind of lead-in in the text tells the reader that a quotation or citation or allusion is about to be presented and that a brief reference in parentheses will tell the reader where to look in the "Works Cited" page(s) for full bibliographic information about the source of that quotation, citation, or allusion.

There are other, mainly mechanical, changes in the new MLA style of documentation:

1. Arabic numerals, rather than Roman numerals, are used to indicate the volume numbers of books as well as journals. Roman numerals, however, are still used (a) to identify a person in a series, for example, Henry VIII, Pope John XXIII, and (b) to cite the pages in the preliminary section of a book, for example, viii, xiv.

2. The abbreviations **p.** (for *page*) and **pp.** (for *pages*) have been eliminated before page numbers, even when no volume number is given.

3. The abbreviations l. (for *line*) and ll. (for *lines*) have been eliminated before line numbers.

4. The comma after the title of a journal has been eliminated, for example, *German Quarterly* 34 (1961).

5. A colon separates the volume number (and date) from the page number, for example, 97 (1986): 88–97.

6. For journals that begin each issue with page 1, the volume number and issue number are given, for example, *American-German Review* 20.4 (1954): 9–10. Sometimes, however, it might be desirable to give the month or the season also, for example, 58.2 (May 1964): 113–14, or 30.3 (Winter 1993): 87.

7. The place of publication is given as it is spelled on the title page or the copyright page. Therefore, sometimes the foreign name of a city rather than the Anglicized name is given in the bibliographical reference, for example, *Praha* for Prague, *Braunschweig* for Brunswick. In some cases, however, it might be useful to give the Anglicized spelling of the city in brackets, for example, Köln [Cologne].

Model parenthetical citations

The general principle governing parenthetical documentation is that only as much additional information should be given within the parentheses as is necessary to enable the reader to determine the source of the quotation or citation or allusion. For instance, if the lead-in for a quotation in the text supplies the name of the author and if only one work by that author is given on the "Works Cited" page at the end of the paper, only the page number of the quoted work needs to be given in the parentheses. (See the following examples.)

1. Author cited in the lead-in:

61

> Travis says that jazz was incubated in Chicago, even though it was not conceived there (8-9).

2. Author not cited in the lead-in:

> Jazz was incubated in Chicago, even though it was not conceived there (Travis 8-9).

3. Two or three authors:

> Logan and Cohen credit the Niagara Movement with being the first successful organized effort of the Negro protest in the twentieth century (164).

4. More than three authors:

> "Popular sovereignty" meant that settlers could vote for or against slavery at the first meeting of their territorial legislature (Divine et al. 384-85).

5. Unknown authorship:

> In architecture, integration of the arts should complement the architectural forms and enhance the total environment (Conrad Schmitt Studies).

6. Two or more works by the same author:

Hollywood, or a segment of it at least, was becoming increasingly active on the question of
civil rights (Baldwin, No Name in the Street
132).

Some argue that a people cannot have a future
until they accept their past (Baldwin, The Fire
Next Time 95).

61

(**Note:** Shortened versions of titles are acceptable, e.g., *No Name* or *Fire*.)

7. Multivolume work:

Other and more serious problems than trans-
portation were raised by the westward movement
after the war (Morison and Commager 1: 441).

8. Government document or corporate author:

The Commission on Law Enforcement and Administration of Justice concluded that there is far
more crime than is ever reported (v).

9. A novel:

Melville's narrator describes Captain Ahab as
having "an eternal anguish in his face" (90;
ch. 28).

10. A poem:

An example of personification is Tennyson's
"broad stream in his banks complaining"
(Shalott 4.120).

11. A play:

```
They were, in fact, "a pair of star-crossed
lovers" (Romeo and Juliet Prologue 6).
```

12. An interview:

```
When questioned about how wise it is for actors
to take work doing commercials, my friend ex-
pressed no concern that the practice would
jeopardize his career (Lordan).
```

13. Citing an entire work:

In a citation of an entire work, rather than just a part of the work, it is preferred that the author's name be included in the text, not in a parenthetical reference.

```
Fleming uses this kind of approach through Arts
& Ideas.
```

Endnotes/footnotes

In cases where several sources are cited and it is necessary to indicate volume numbers, page numbers, multiple authors, and so on, an endnote (or footnote) should be used. Clearly, the following citation would be intrusive and disruptive if included in your text:

```
(Holmes 118-22; Sims and Bates 1: 233-34; Whit-
field iv-vii; Ray 97; Scott et al. 512-14)
```

A superscript numeral is used in the text to direct the reader to the page titled **Notes** at the end or to a footnote that appears at the bottom of the page. You can include two or more works in a single parenthetical reference simply by separating them with a semicolon:

```
(Kepler 616; Alvarez 98-102)
```

Works cited

In a research paper, the bibliography is placed at the end of the paper. It is there that the researcher provides full information about all the sources used in the paper. Start on a new page and proceed as follows:

1. The heading **Works Cited** should be centered, one inch down from the top of the page.
2. Double-space between the heading and the first entry.
3. Begin the first entry flush with the left-hand margin. If an entry requires more than one line, indent all subsequent lines five spaces from the left margin.
4. Double-space between and within entries, and continue the list for as many pages as necessary.

61

Alphabetize the entries by the author's last name or, if the work is anonymous, according to the first letter of the first significant word in the title. For example, *A Handbook of Korea* is alphabetized under *H*. Underlining (instead of italicizing) is acceptable for book titles.

1. A single book by a single author:

Seki, Hozen. The Great Natural Way. New York: American
    Buddhist Academy, 1976.

2. A single book by more than one author:

Baran, Paul A., and Paul M. Sweezy. Monopoly Capital:
    An Essay on American Economic and Social Order.
    New York: Monthly Review P, 1966.

3. A book of more than one volume:

Hays, William Lee, and Robert L. Winkler. Statistics:
    Probability, Inference, and Decision. 2 vols. New
    York: Holt, 1970.

4. A book edited by one or more editors:

Smith, David Nicol, ed. <u>The Letters of Jonathan Swift
to Charles Ford</u>. Oxford: Clarendon, 1935.

Connors, Robert J., Lisa Ede, and Andrea Lunsford, eds.
<u>Essays on Classical Rhetoric and Modern Discourse</u>.
Carbondale: Southern Illinois UP, 1984.

61

5. An essay or a chapter by an author in an edited collection:

Gordon, Mary. "The Parable of the Cave." <u>The Writer on
Her Work</u>. Ed. Janet Sternburg. New York: Norton,
1980. 27-32.

6. A new edition of a book:

Doughty, Oswald. <u>A Victorian Romantic, Dante Gabriel
Rosetti</u>. 2nd ed. London: Oxford UP, 1960.

7. A book that is part of a series:

Heytesbury, William. <u>Medieval Logic and the Rise of
Mathematical Physics</u>. University of Wisconsin Publications in Medieval Science. Madison: U of Wisconsin P, 1956.

8. A book in a paperback series:

Keillor, Garrison. <u>WLT: A Radio Romance</u>. New York: Pen-
guin Books, 1992.

9. A translation:

Dostoevsky, Fyodor. <u>Crime and Punishment</u>. Trans. Con-
stance Garnet. New York: Heritage, 1938.

10. A signed and an unsigned article from an encyclopedia:

Ewing, J. A. "Steam Engine and Other Heat-Engines."
    Encyclopaedia Britannica. 9th ed. 1980.

"Dwarfed Trees." Encyclopedia Americana. 1948.

11. An article from a journal:

Nelms, Gerald. "The Rise of Classical Rhetoric in
    Modern Composition Studies." Focuses 8.1 (Summer
    1995): 3-30.

61

12. An article in a popular magazine:

Morganthau, Tom, and Seema Nayyar. "Those Scary College
    Costs." Newsweek 29 Apr. 1996: 52-6.

13. A signed and an unsigned article in a newspaper:

Sanger, David E. "Dollar Continues to Plunge as U.S.
    Ponders Strategy." New York Times. 7 Mar. 1995,
    late ed.: A1+.

"Estonia's Government Is Ousted in Vote Signaling Slower
    Reform." New York Times 7 Mar. 1995, late ed.: A10.

14. A signed book review:

Royster, Jacqueline Jones. "New Histories of Rhetoric."
    College English 58 (Feb. 1996): 219-24.

15. A government booklet or pamphlet:

United States. Social Security Administration. Aid to
    Families with Dependent Children: 1973 Recipient
    Characteristics Study. Washington: GPO, 1975.

16. A personal letter or interview:

Glenn, Senator John. Letter to the author, 20 June
      1983.

Herrens, Malcolm B. Telephone interview, 3 Feb. 1980.

17. A recording or jacket notes:

Seeger, Pete, and Arlo Guthrie. "Joe Hill." <u>Together in
      Concert</u>. L.P. Warner, 1975.

18. A film, a radio program, or a television program:

<u>Tootsie</u>. Screenplay by Don McGuire and Larry Gelbart.
      Dir. Sydney Pollack. Perf. Dustin Hoffman, Jessica
      Lange, and Terri Garr. Mirage/Punch Production.
      Columbia, 1982.

Sample Paper—MLA Style

Eileen Diaz   Diaz 1

ENC 1102

Professor Janice Walker

April 1, 1996

Anorexia and Bulimia: Societal Diseases

Women in our society suffer from many "stres-
sors," including personal and cultural values, genetic
disorders, and family relationships. These factors may
manifest themselves in the physical symptoms typical of
anorexia and bulimia, such as depression, weight problems, and obsessive dieting. Our society glamorizes the
look of the Barbie doll and the waiflike look of the
high-fashion model. Unfortunately, these portrayals of
the "perfect figure" have caused serious problems. To
fully understand the effects of eating disorders such
as anorexia nervosa and bulimia on young women, we must
look at the underlying causes of the diseases.

Anorexia nervosa is a "disruption in the normal
eating habits characterized by an all-consuming fear of
becoming fat" (Wildes). Anorexics starve themselves in
order to gain control of their bodies. Quite often,
people with anorexia will also deny that they have a
problem. Closely related to anorexia is bulimia, a
"cycle of uncontrolled binge eating followed by purging

through vomiting or the use of laxatives" (Wildes). According to Alice Tobias, "bulimics have a morbid fear of becoming fat" (174). Many anorexics also show some bulimic behavior, and bulimics usually go through an anorexic phase or demonstrate anorexic behavior. Both anorexics and bulimics are excessively concerned with their weight and with food. "In a society blessed with food for all," says Judith Gordon, "increasing numbers of people, particularly teenage girls, starve themselves by choice" (147). Both of these diseases can cause serious physical harm. Why would otherwise healthy women choose literally to starve themselves to death?

Being overweight is considered ugly and undesirable. It does not fit with our society's definition of being feminine: "Women are expected to be petite, demure, giving, passive, receptive in the home and above all, attractive" (Orbach 168). While many women strongly protest this demeaning portrayal, it is the standard the insecure woman lives by. Magazines are filled with the emaciated bodies of models who are supposedly the epitome of beauty and femininity. Many young women strive to become like those supermodels, whose pictures they see plastered everywhere, not realizing the detrimental effect on their health. Our so-

ciety emphasizes being thin and losing weight; thin
means beautiful, intelligent, and capable of achieving
any goal. Females typically feel more stress than males
to conform to the physical stereotypes because "they
are brought up to conform to an image of womanhood that
places importance on body size and shape" (14). Food
becomes an enemy, a nemesis that they must overpower by
not eating or by purging themselves when they do eat.

Researchers have begun to suspect that there may
also be a connection between eating disorders and genetics. An article in Mademoiselle showed that women
with these eating disorders usually have a family
member who suffers from depression, alcoholism, or an
eating disorder (Kirschhoch 165). By determining the
gene that is believed to control eating disorders, many
researchers believe that improved methods of treatment
can be found to better assist and understand the people
affected. A gene is a carrier of hereditary character-
istics that are passed from parents to their children.
Isolating the gene could prove invaluable to both the
study and the treatment of anorexia and bulimia.

Our society's attitudes toward obesity contribute
to the problem as well. Many of the explanations for
obesity "point a finger at the failure of women themselves to control their weight, control their ap-

Diaz 4

petites, and control their impulses" (Orbach 16). This
attitude contributes to the pressure on young women to
be thin, to prove they are in control of themselves and
their bodies. It is the distortion of the concept of
the body (that only thin people are good) that leads
many young women to slowly self-destruct. "Fat is a social disease," says Ohrbach, that many young women grow
up dealing with (18). Regrettably, some take more
drastic measures than others. The pressures of society,
the stereotypes and peer pressure to conform to unreal-
istic standards of beauty, can be deadly.

Many people with eating disorders are insecure and
depend on the perceptions of others. They want to be
accepted, and they want a sense of being in control. By
not eating, anorexics express a power over their
bodies. This excessive need for power and acceptance
and the drastic measures taken to attain them can be
deadly. We need more research into the possible genetic
causes of obesity and eating disorders such as anorexia
and bulimia. We also need to recognize that there is no
one perfect image of beauty--that beautiful women come
in all shapes and sizes. And we need to find ways to
bolster the self-esteem of young women that are not defined by some misguided stereotype of femininity. "Men

act and women appear," says Ohrbach--this is what our
society expects (19). Positive role models for women
and realistic portrayals of the female body can help
women in our society to value themselves as worthwhile
human beings rather than as mere Barbie dolls.

Diaz 6

Works Cited

Gordon, Judith Bograd. "To Eat or Not to Eat: Toward a Sociology of Anorexia." Evaluation and Management of Eating Disorders. Eds. William Castelli, Kristine Clark, and Richard Parr. Champaign, IL: Life Enhancement, 1988.

Kirschhoch, Claudia A. "Dying for a Candy Bar." Mademoiselle. Mar. 1996: 164+.

Orbach, Susie. Fat Is a Feminist Issue . . . The Anti-Diet Guide to Permanent Weight Loss. New York: Paddington, 1978.

Tobias, Alice L. "Bulimia: An Overview." Evaluation and Management of Eating Disorders. Eds. William Castelli, Kristine Clark, and Richard Parr. Champaign, IL: Life Enhancement, 1988.

Wildes, Cheryl A. "What Are Eating Disorders?" http://www.neca.com/~cwildes/index.htm. 23 Mar. 1996.

62 Documenting Electronic Sources in the MLA Style

The following models demonstrate the guidelines for citing electronic sources according to the 1998 *MLA Style Manual and Guide to Scholarly Publishing*. The MLA recommends these general conventions:

PUBLICATION DATES For sources taken from the Internet, include the date the source was posted to the Internet or last updated or revised; give also the date the source was accessed.

62

UNIFORM RESOURCE LOCATOR (URL) Include a full and accurate URL for any source taken from the Internet (with access-mode identifier—*http, ftp, gopher,* or *telenet*). Enclose URLs in angle brackets (< >). When URL continues from one line to the next, break it only after a slash. Do not add a hyphen.

PAGE NUMBERING Include page or paragraph numbers when given by the source

When citing electronic sources, follow the formatting conventions illustrated by the following models:

An online scholarly project or database

The Walt Whitman Hypertext Archive. Eds. Kenneth

    M. Price and Ed Folsom. 16 Mar. 1998. College of

    William and Mary. 3 Apr.1998

    <http://jefferson.village.Virginia.EDU/whitman/>.

1. Title of project or database
2. Name of the editor of project
3. Electronic publication information
4. Date of access and URL

A short work within a scholarly project

Whitman, Walt. "Crossing Brooklyn Ferry." The Walt

    Whiteman Hypertext Archive. Eds. Kenneth M. Price

and Ed Folsom. 16 Mar. 1 998. College of William
and Mary. 3 Apr. 1998
<http://jefferson.village.Virginia.EDU/whitman/
works/leaves/1891/text/index.html>.

An online book published independently

Smith, Adam. The Wealth of Nations. New York: Methuen,
1994. 3 Mar. 1998.
<http://www.mk.net/-dt/Bibliomania/NonFiction/
Smith/Wealth/index.html>.

1. Author's name
2. Title of the work
3. Name of the editor, compiler, or translator
4. Publication information
5. Date of access and URL

An article in a scholarly journal

Jackson, Francis L. "Mexican Freedom: The Ideal of the
Indigenous State." Animus 2-3 (1997) 4 Apr. 1998
<http://www.mun.ca/animus/1997vol2/jackson2.htm>.

1. Author's name
2. Title of the work or material in quotation marks
3. Name of periodical
4. Volume number, issue number, or other identifying number
5. Date of publication
6. Page numbers or number of paragraphs, pages, or other numbered sections (if any)
7. Date of access and URL

An editorial or letter to the editor

"The Net Escape Censorship? Ha!" Editorial. Wired 3.09.
1 Apr. 1998

    <http://www.wired.com/wired/3.09/departments/
    baker.if.<html>.

A periodical source on CD-ROM, diskette, or magnetic tape

Ellis, Richard. "Whale Killing Begins Anew." <u>Audobon</u>
    [GAUD] 94.6 (1992); 20-22. <u>General Periodicals
    Ondisc-Magazine Express. CD-ROM.</u> UMI-Proquest. 1992.

1. Author's name
2. Publication information for analogous printed source (title and date)
3. Title of database
4. Publication medium
5. Nameofvendor
6. Date of electronic publication

62

A non-periodical source on CD-ROM, diskette, or magnetic tape

Clements, John. "War of 1812." <u>Chronology of the United
    States</u>. CD-ROM. Dallas: Political Research, Inc. 1997

1. Author's, editor's, compiler's, or translator's name (if given)
2. Part ofwork being cited
3. Title ofthe publication
4. Name ofthe editor, compiler, or translator (if relevant)
5. Publication medium
6. Edition, release, or version
7. Place of publication
8. Name of publisher
9. Date of publication

A personal or professional site

Winter, Mick. <u>How to Talk New Age. 6 Apr. 1998</u>
<http//www.mk.net/dt/BibliomaniaNonFiction/Smith/Wealth/
    index.html>.

An article in a magazine

Pitta, Julie. "Un-Wired?" <u>Forbes</u> 20 Apr. 1998. 20 Apr.
    1998.
        <http://www.forbes.com/Forbes/98/0420/6108045a.htm>.

An abstract

Maia, Ana Couto. "Prospects for United Nations Peace-
    keeping: Lessons from the Congo Experience." <u>MAI</u>
    36.2 (1998): 400. Abstract. 6 Apr. 1998
    (http://wwwlib.umi.com/dissertations/
    fullcit?289845?

Usenet

Dorsey, Michael. R. "Environmentalism or Racism." 25
    Mar. 1998. Online posting. 1 Apr. 1998
        <news:alt.org.sierra-club>.

Electronic mail

Mendez, Michael R. "Re: Solar power." E-mail to Edgar
    V. Atamian. 11 Sept. 1996.

Walker, Janice R. "Electronic Documentation." Personal
    e-mail. 12 May 1996.

63 The APA System

Just as the MLA system of documentation is predominant in the humanities, the APA system is predominant in such fields as psychology,
education, psycholinguistics, and many of the social sciences. Over 200
scholarly journals in the United States now prescribe the APA style of
documentation. The highlights of this system will be presented

here; for a fuller treatment, consult the readily available paperback edition of *Publication Manual of the American Psychological Association,* 4th ed., Washington, DC: American Psychological Association, 1994.

The principal difference between the MLA and the APA systems is that the MLA in-text and parenthetical citations feature the name of the author and the location of the information; the APA citations feature the name of the author, the date, and the location. The date is featured in scientific writing for the obvious reason that a researcher must present the most up-to-date information that is available.

Here is how the first in-text reference to a book would be documented, first in the MLA style and then in the APA style. (Note that in the parentheses, the APA retains the abbreviations *p.* and *pp.* and puts a comma between the author's name and the date of publication.)

63

1. Author cited in the lead-in:

MLA

```
Tracy defended the "big-bang" theory (234).
```

APA

```
Tracy (1985) defended the "big bang" theory (p.
234).
```

2. Author not cited in the lead-in:

MLA

```
The "big bang" theory can be defended (Tracy
234)
```

APA

```
The "big bang" theory can be defended (Tracy,
1985, p. 234).
```

Readers who want fuller information about the work cited in the APA parenthetical reference can turn to the list of references at the end of the paper. There, in an alphabetical listing, the Tracy work would be entered in doublespaced typescript as follows:

```
Tracy, A. (1985). New theories on the origins
     of the universe. New York: Downey.
```

Variations on the basic APA style of documentation

63

1. If a whole work is being referred to, only the author's last name and the date of the work are given in parentheses.

   ```
   A recent study has confirmed that 12-year-
   olds grow at an amazingly rapid rate
   (Swanson, 1969).
   ```

2. A page number or a chapter number is supplied only if only part of a work is being referred to. Quotations always demand the addition of a page number.

   ```
   The committee boldly declared that "morality
   could not be enforced, but it could be
   bought" (Dawson, 1975, p. 105).
   ```

3. Any information supplied in the text itself need not be repeated in the parentheses.

   ```
   Anderson (1948) found that only middle-class
   Europeans disdained our cultural values.

   In 1965, Miller professed his fervent admira-
   tion of our admissions policy.
   ```

4. If a work has two authors, both authors (connected by an ampersand) should be cited each time a reference is made to that particular text. If a work has three to five authors, all the authors should be cited the first time, but subsequently only the name of the first author followed by **et al.** needs to be given. For six or

more authors, even in the first citation of the work, give only the first author's name, followed by "et al."

```
The circulation of false rumors poisoned the
environment of that conference (Getty &
Howard, 1979).

The overall effect of the smear tactics was a
marked decline in voter registrations
(Abraham, Davis, & Keppler, 1952).

In three successive national elections,
voters from Slavic neighborhoods showed a 72%
turnout (Abraham et al., 1952, pp. 324-327).
```

63

5. If several works are cited in parentheses at the same point in the text, the works should be arranged alphabetically according to the last name of the first author and should be separated by semicolons.

```
All the studies of the problem agree that the
proposed remedy is worse than the malady
(Brown & Turkell, 1964; Firkins, 1960; How-
ells, 1949; Jackson, Miller, & Naylor, un-
dated; Kameron, in press).
```

6. If several works by the same author are cited in the same reference, the works are distinguished by the publication dates, arranged in chronological order and separated by commas. Two or more works published by the same author in the same year are distinguished by the letters **a, b, c,** and so on, added to the repeated date. In such chronological listings, works "in press" are always listed last.

```
A consistent view on this point has been re-
peatedly expressed by the Canadian member of
```

```
the commission (Holden, 1959, 1965, 1970,
1971a, 1971b, 1976).
```

7. If no author is given for a work, two or three words from another part of the entry (usually from the title) should be used to refer to the work.

```
The voters' apathy was decried in the final
spring meeting of the city council ("The
Gradual Decline," 1976).
```

63

List of references

The "References" page appended to a paper that observes the APA style is comparable to, and yet different from, the "Works Cited" page in a paper that observed the MLA style. Both systems give full bibliographic information about the works cited in the body of the writing, and both systems arrange the entries alphabetically according to the last name of the author. In both systems, the names of the authors are inverted (surname first), but in the APA system, only the initials of the first and middle names are given, and when there are two or more authors of a work, the names of *all* the authors are inverted.

The conventions of sequence, punctuation, and capitalization in the APA style for the references section can most easily be illustrated with examples.

1. A book by a single author:

```
Chang, S. T. (1976). The complete book of acupuncture.
    Milbrae, CA: Celestial Arts.
```

The title of the book is underlined, and only the first word of the title and the first word following a colon (if there is a colon) in the title are capitalized. (Any proper nouns in a title would also be capitalized; see the following example.) The three main parts of an entry—author, title, and publication data—are separated with a period and one space.

2. A book by several authors:

Koslin, S., Koslin, B. L., Parganent, R., & Pendelton, S. (1975). An evaluation of fifth-grade reading programs in ten New York City Community School Districts, 1973-1974. New York: Riverside Research Institute.

63

Note that the names of all the authors are inverted, that the names are separated by commas, and that an ampersand (**&**) is put before the last name in the series (even when there are only two names; see the following example).

3. An article in an edited collection:

Bobrow, D. G., & Norman, D. A. (1975). Some principles of memory schemata. In D. G. Bobrow & A. M. Collins (Eds.), Representation and understanding: Studies in cognitive science. New York: Academic Press.

Note that the title of the article (**Some principles ...**) is not enclosed in quotation marks and that only the first word of this title is capitalized. (Any proper nouns in the title of the article would, of course, be capitalized.) Note also that the subsequent names of the two editors (**Eds.**) of the collection are not inverted and that there is no comma between the names.

4. An article in a journal:

Stahl, A. (1977). The structure of children's compositions: Developmental and ethnic differences. Research in the Teaching of English, 11, 156-163.

Note that all substantive words in the title of the journal are capitalized and that the title of the journal is underlined. Note also that the year comes after the author's name and that the volume number (*11*) is underlined. For a journal that begins the numbering of its pages with page 1 in each issue, the number of the issue should be indicated with an Arabic number following the volume number in parentheses, with no space between them: *11*(**3**).

63

5. A book by a corporate author:

```
American Psychological Association. (1966). Standards
    for educational and psychological texts and
    manuals. Washington, DC: Author.
```

Books and authors with corporate authors are listed alphabetically according to the first significant word of the entry (here, **American**). The word **Author** indicates that the publisher of the work is the same as the group named in the author slot. If, however, the publisher is different from the corporate author, the name of the publisher should be given right after the place of publication.

These five models cover most of the kinds of published material likely to be used in a research paper. For additional models, consult the *Publication Manual of the American Psychological Association,* 4th ed., Washington, DC: American Psychological Association, 1994.

For an illustration of the physical appearance, in typescript, of a research paper and of references done according to the APA system of documentation, see the following pages, taken from a 26-page article by George E. Newell of Ohio State University, "Reader-Based and Teacher-Centered Instructional Tasks: Writing and Learning About a Short Story in Middle-Track Classrooms," in *Journal of Literacy Research,* Volume 28, Number 1, 1996, pages 147–172. Please note that in the references on page 204 we have included only those sources that are cited in the following excerpt. The article, in its entirety, included 37 entries in its references.

Sample Paper—APA Style

Reader-Based and Teacher-Centered Instructional Tasks:

Writing and Learning About a Short Story

in Middle-Track Classrooms

George E. Newell

Ohio State University

Reader-Based and Teacher-Centered Instructional Tasks:

Writing and Learning About a Short Story

in Middle-Track Classrooms

At some point in high school, students from all
instructional tracks engage in discussions of and
writing about literature. Although we currently know
little about what such activities contribute to student
learning in particular tracks, Applebee (1993) clearly
demonstrates that sheer quantity of discussion and
writing are central to literature instruction. Ninety-
one percent of the public-school teachers reported "or-
ganizing class discussions" as the most highly rated
instructional technique, and 82% reported the essay as
the most typical writing assignment assigned in representative classes. Given their ubiquity in the English
classroom, it seems remarkable that we have only a
slender body of empirical research exploring the consequences of discussion and writing for students' literary understanding (Marshall, 1987; Marshall,
Smagorinsky, & Smith, 1995; Newell, Suszynski, & Weingart, 1989). Furthermore, we have even fewer studies of
literature instruction focused on high-school students
in instructional tracks other than college-preparatory
classrooms (Marshall et al., 1995).

The importance of conducting instructional research in all tracks (upper, middle, and lower) was
made clear in a recent study of classroom discussions
of literature (Marshall et al., 1995). For example, although Marshall et al.'s (1995) study suggests that
middle-track students had a wide range of abilities and
attitudes, the discourse patterns in these classroom
discussions were fundamentally similar to the patterns
in the discussions in all three tracks, including
upper-track classrooms. "The teacher ultimately controlled the direction, the pace, and the organization
in most of the discussions we observed" (Marshall et
al., 1995, p. 55). In spite of the range of abilities
in middle-track classes, the teachers did not seem to
have developed more reader-based approaches (e.g.,
small-group work and process-oriented writing activities) that may provide for more individualized instruction, a pattern similar to the practices of teachers of
mixed-ability classrooms that Applebee (1993) surveyed
in his national study.

If teachers are asked to shift the emphasis in instruction from the teacher and the text to the students
and the process of understanding, then literature research must provide analyses of the problems and bene-

fits that might be expected, as well as models for re-
considering instructional tasks. Middle-track literature
classrooms are particularly demanding for teachers who
may feel they must lead oftentimes passive students to a
"proper" reading. Even if their literature teachers do
try to challenge middle-track students academically,
these students may not have an appropriate degree of
skill to acquire some measure of success.

How then might we rethink instruction in a way that
both challenges and instructs middle-track students in
the study of literary texts? In recent years, many new
developments in reader-response theory have emerged from
Rosenblatt's (1978) earlier argument concerning the need
to return the student to the center of the instructional
enterprise. Her transactional theory of reading has become a model of literature instruction--reading as a
"quiet converation" with books. Such a conversation
would include students' examinations of their own trans-
actions with texts and an exploration of how the text
and their experiences fostered their responses.

Although Rosenblatt's work offers broad principles
for the nature and significance of literary education,
it offers few practical guidelines for the enactment of
"quiet conversations" within the realities of classroom
life. Moreover, we have ample evidence that literature
teachers are typically concerned with an academic ap-

proach that focuses on how a text "works." A fundamental assumption operating in many literature classrooms is that the author's meaning remains hidden until
unveiled by the teacher's own interpretive agenda (Applebee, 1993; Purves, 1981). As one perspective among
many possibilities, this assumption does not pose a
problem. In the case of middle-track students, however,
if Marshall et al.'s (1995) descriptions are at all
representative, these students need instruction in the
inquiry process with more explicit attention to making
sense of their own understandings.

. . .

Instructional Tasks   6

References

Applebee, A. N. (1993). <u>Literature in the secondary school</u> (Research Report No. 25). Urbana, IL: National Council of Teachers of English.

Marshall, J. D. (1987). The effects of writing on students' understanding of literary texts. <u>Research in the Teaching of English, 21,</u> 30-63.

Marshall, J. D., Smagorinsky, P., & Smith, M. (1995). <u>The language of interpretation: Patterns of discourse in discussions of literature</u> (Research Report No. 27). Urbana, IL: National Council of Teachers of English.

Newell, G. E., Suszynski, K., & Weingart, R. (1989). The effects of writing in a reader-based and text-based mode on students' understanding of two short stories. <u>Journal of Reading Behavior, 21,</u> 37-57.

Purves, A. (1981). <u>Reading and literature.</u> Urbana, IL: National Council of Teachers of English.

Rosenblatt, L. (1978). <u>The reader, the text, the poem.</u> Carbondale, IL: Southern Illinois University Press.

64 The CBE System

Since we have displayed the documentation system that prevails in the humanities (the **MLA** system) and the documentation system that prevails in the social sciences (the **APA** system), we are now going to display the **CBE** system, the documentation system that prevails in such biological sciences as anatomy, biochemistry, biology, genetics, physiology, and zoology. These three systems are more similar than different. For a complete set of CBE models of how to cite references in the text and how to list references in the bibliography at the end of the paper, consult *Scientific Style and Format: The CBE Manual for Authors, Editors, and Publishers,* 6th ed., Bethesda, MD: Council of Biology Editors, 1994. But here are the basic CBE forms of the parenthetical references in the text of your paper and of the complete listing of references at the end of your paper.

64

In the text, only the last name of the author(s) and the publication date of the reference are given:

One author:

```
Ferguson (1978) or (Ferguson 1978)
```

Two authors:

```
Martineau and Bouret (1986) or (Martineau and
Bouret 1986)
```

Three or more authors:

```
Henderson et al. (1995) or (Henderson et al.
1995)
```

The placement of the parentheses depends on the structure of your sentence:

```
Ferguson (1978) has confirmed these findings in
his later study.
```

```
The confirmation of this experiment came from
two of the professor's graduate students (Hen-
derson et al. 1995).

Martineau and Bouret (1986, p 34) firmly main-
tained that "an infusion of oxygen would utterly
invalidate the experimenter's findings."
```

The latter illustration demonstrates that sometimes, especially when you are referring to only a part of a book or an article or when you are quoting from a text, you should add the page number(s) to the name of the author(s) and the date:

```
Isaacson (1991, p 318) or (Isaacson 1991, p
318).

Forbes et al. (1945, p 91-105) or Forbes et al.
1945, p 91-105).
```

If you cannot find the name of the author(s) or you can find only a corporate author, here is how you enter the citation:

```
Anonymous (1980, p 6-8) or (Anonymous 1980, p
6-8) or (CBE Style Manual Committee 1994, p
48).
```

Some journals just assign a number to a reference, depending on the order of the reference in the text, and some journals, in addition to the assigned number, supply the name of the author(s).

```
These results were later confirmed in Prague.[4]
```

Of course, in the bibliographic section of the paper, all the bibliographic information about these references is supplied, but sometimes, these numbered references are listed there not in alphabetical order but in the exact order in which they occur in the text.

If the author(s) and the date of two or more references are identical, put a lowercase letter a, b, c, and so on after the dates:

```
McNamara (1992a), McNamara (1992b), McNamara
(1992c)
```

In the bibliographic section at the end of the paper, those three references would be listed in the a, b, c order.

List of references

64

Whereas in the in-text citations only the last name of the author(s), the date, and sometimes the page number(s) are given, the complete bibliographic information is supplied in the bibliography section at the end of the paper: the full name of the author(s), the title of the article or book, the place of publication, the publishers, and the date of publication, volume number, and inclusive page numbers.

For the name(s) of the author(s), only the surname and then the initials of the given names are used, and if there are two or more authors, the names are separated by semicolons.

The titles of books are not italicized, and the titles of articles are not enclosed in quotation marks; only the first word and any proper nouns in the titles are capitalized; and the titles of journals are not italicized and are usually abbreviated, unless the title is a one-word title (e.g., *Science*).

The edition of a book is given (e.g., 3rd ed.) if it is an edition other than the first. If the book was published in more than one volume, the number of volumes (e.g., 3 vol.) must be noted after the publication date, the place of publication, and the publisher are given.

For journal articles, the following information is supplied after the title of the article: the title of the journal, which is abbreviated, unless it is a one-word title; the date of the issue, followed by a semicolon (e.g., 1992;) the volume number of the issue (in an Arabic numeral—e.g., 89), followed by a colon (e.g., 89:); the inclusive page numbers of the article with duplicated digits omitted (e.g., 122–8), followed by a period. So here is the sequence of the information given after the title of an article: **J Cell Biol 1976; 89: 122–8.**

The bibliography page of the research paper should bear some title, such as "List of References," "Literature Cited," or "References Cited." If the entries under this title are not numbered, they are listed alphabetically according to the last name of the first author listed; the first line of each entry starts flush with the left-hand margin; and all subsequent lines of the entry are indented two spaces from the lefthand margin.

64

Here, in typescript, is an extended quotation from a two-volume book by Thomas Hall, and following that in-text quotation is an alphabetized "List of References," which contains a variety of entries in the CBE style of documentation, including the entry for Thomas Hall's book:

```
Hall (1969) summarizes the differing views of

Plato and Aristotle about the cause of the natural

order in this fashion:

    Plato and Aristotle both concerned them-

    selves, then, with the causes of natural

    order. Order arises in Plato's system out of

    the interplay of (a) reason and (b) neces-

    sity. In Aristotle's system, it arises out of

    the interplay of material, efficient, formal,

    and final causes. Occasionally, Aristotle

    borrows the terminology of his teacher and

    refers to material and efficient causation,
```

taken together, as necessity. And frequently,
he acknowledges that his formal and final
causes are almost indistinguishable from one
another (1:118).

List of References

[Anonymous]. Epidemiology for primary health care. Int
    J Epidemiol 1976;5:224-5.

Baldwin KM. Cardiac gap junction configuration after an
    uncoupling treatment as a function of time. J Cell
    Bio 1979;82:66-75.

De Robertis ECP, Saez FA, De Robertis EMF, Jr. 1975.
    Cell biology. 6th ed. Philadelphia: WB Saunders.

Gardner JD, Jensen RT. 1981. Regulation of pancreatic
    enzyme secretion in vitro. In: LR Johnson, editor.
    Physiology of the gastrointestinal tract. New
    York: Haven Press. 831-71.

Hall TS. Ideas of life and matter: studies in the his-
    tory of general physiology, 600 B.C.-1900 A.D.
    1969: Chicago: Univ Chicago Press, 2 vol.

Olive LS. The genus Protostelium. Am J Bot 1962;49:
    297-303.

White HB. III. Coenzymes as fossils of an earlier mole-
    cular state. J Mol Evol 1976;7:101-4.

64

65 The Chicago System

The *Manual of Style,* first published by the University of Chicago Press in 1906, is probably the oldest of the style manuals in the United States. In 1982, with the publication of the thirteenth edition, this manual added the word *Chicago* to the title and became *The Chicago Manual of Style.* In 1993, the fourteenth edition of *The Chicago Manual of Style* was published. For undergraduate students, the condensed version of this manual—a book that we mentioned earlier, Kate L. Turabian's *A Manual for Writers of Term Papers, Theses, and Dissertations,* now in its sixth edition—is a more suitable guide to the Chicago system of documentation. We are presenting the Chicago system of documentation here because it is the primary guide recommended by those journals that still use footnotes or endnotes for the research articles they publish. We will introduce you here to the footnote method of documenting sources in research papers.

At the end of every quotation or paraphrase in a research paper, put a raised or superscript Arabic numeral (like this[1]) at the end of the sentence. At the bottom of each page, supply a footnote, preceded by the numeral, for the quotation or paraphrase. The first time a source is cited in a paper, the footnote should be full, giving the name of the author(s), the underlined title of the book or, if it is an article in a journal or a collection, the title of the article in quotation marks, the underlined title of the journal or of the book in which the essay appeared, and the appropriate publication information (e.g., place of publication, publisher, date of publication, volume number, and page numbers).

Here are the directions for the format of the footnotes.

1. Single-space each footnote, but double-space between each footnote.
2. The footnotes should be numbered consecutively throughout the paper.

3. The first line of every footnote, preceded by its number, should be indented five spaces.
4. At the bottom of the page, there should be a footnote for every superscript on that page.
5. Separate the text and the footnote(s) on every page with a 12-space line that begins at the left-hand margin.
6. The name(s) of the author(s) should not be inverted but should appear in the regular order.

Here are some model footnotes in the Chicago style.

65

1. Footnote for a journal article:

1. Richard Straub, "The Concept of Control in Teacher Response: Defining the Varieties of 'Directive' and 'Facilitative' Commentary," CCC 47 (May 1996): 223-4.

2. Footnote for an article in a book or collection:

2. Kenneth Burke, "The Allies of Humanism Abroad," in A Critique of Humanism, ed. Hartley Grattan (New York: Brewer and Warren, 1930), 169-70.

3. Footnote for a book:

3. Mina P. Shaughnessy, Errors and Expectations (New York: Oxford University Press, 1977), 35.

4. Footnote for an edition that has more than three authors:

4. Albert C. Baugh et al., A Literary History of England, 2nd ed. (New York: Appleton, 1967), 243-5.

5. Footnote for a magazine article:

5. Roger Angell, "Conic Projection," The New Yorker, 20 May 1996, 49-50.

6. Footnote for a newspaper article:

        6. William Robbins, "Big Wheels: The Rotary Club
at 75," <u>New York Times</u>, 17 February 1980, sec. 3.

66 Other Documentation Systems

Most of the scholarly disciplines specify the style of documentation that they prefer, and when you begin to major in one of those disciplines, you will be expected to use that style of documentation in the research papers or articles that you write. In the masthead of professional journals, the editor usually indicates what system of documentation authors should observe in the articles they submit for consideration. Here is a list of a few more documentation systems:

<u>ACS Style Guide: A Manual for Authors and Editors</u>. Ed.
        J. S. Dodd. Washington, DC: American Chemical So-
        ciety, 1985.

<u>AIP Style Manual for Guidance in Preparation of Papers</u>.
        New York: American Institute of Physics, 1990.

<u>American Medical Association Manual of Style</u>, 8th ed.
        William & Wilkins, 1989.

<u>A Manual for Authors of Mathematical Papers</u>. 8th ed.
        Providence, RI: American Mathematical Society,
        1984; rev. ed. 1990.

None of the expositions of the documentation systems presented in this book will adequately serve those who are seriously engaged in research and publication in their chosen discipline. They will have to acquire the official style manual for their particular discipline and study it carefully. What our abbreviated presentation of the MLA, the APA, the CBE, the ACW, and the Chicago style of documentation can do for undergraduate students is to enable them, with some additional guidance from their instructor, to prepare a properly documented research paper in fulfillment of a course assignment. This entire section on the format of the research paper can serve only to *introduce* a student to the intricacies and the conventions of scholarly research.

Forms for Letters

The one type of writing that most people engage in after leaving school is letter writing. You will almost certainly write letters to parents, friends, and acquaintances, and you may have to write letters in connection with your job. Occasionally, you may feel compelled to write a letter to the editor of a newspaper or magazine, and sometimes, you may write more formal letters to institutions or officials for such purposes as applying for a job, requesting information or a service, or seeking the redress of some grievance. Although you do not have to be much concerned about the niceties of form and etiquette when you are writing to intimate friends, you would be well advised to observe the conventions of form and etiquette in letters addressed to people whom you do not know well enough to call by their first names.

67 Format of Familiar Letter

Letters written to acquaintances are commonly referred to as *familiar letters*. Although usually "anything goes" in letters to acquaintances, you should keep in mind that even the most intimate acquaintance is flattered if the author of the letter observes certain amenities of form. Here is a list of the conventions for the familiar letter:

1. Familiar letters may be written on lined or unlined paper of any size.

2. Familiar letters may be handwritten and may be written on both sides of the sheet of paper. Of course, you could write a familiar letter on a typewriter or on a computer.

3. The author of the letter usually puts his or her address and the date at the right-hand side of the heading but does not, as in a business letter, put at the left-hand side of the heading the name and address of the person to whom the letter is addressed.

4. Depending on the degree of your intimacy with the addressee, you may use salutations like these: **Dear Mom, Dear Jim, Dear Julie, Dear Ms. Worth.** The salutation is often followed by a comma rather than the more formal colon.

5. The body of the letter may be written in indented paragraphs, single- or double-spaced.

6. Depending on the degree of your intimacy with the addressee, you may use complimentary closes like these: **Sincerely, Affectionately, Yours, Much love, Fondly, As ever.**

7. Depending on the degree of your intimacy with the addressee, you may sign your full name or just a first name or a nickname.

68

68 Format of Business Letter

Formal letters addressed to organizations or customers or professionals or executives are commonly called *business letters.* The form of business letters is more strictly prescribed than the form of familiar letters. Models for a business letter appear on pages 218 and 220. Here is a list of the conventions for the business letter:

1. Business letters are written on $8\frac{1}{2}$" × 11" unlined paper or on $8\frac{1}{2}$" × 11" printed letterhead.

2. Business letters must be typewritten, single-spaced, on one side of the paper only.

3. In the sample business letter that is typed on printed letterhead stationery (p. 220), the so-called *full block* format of formal business letters is illustrated. Note that in this format, everything—

date, address, greeting, text, and complimentary close—begins at the left-hand margin. Compare this format with the *semiblock* format of the sample business letter that is typed on plain white paper (p. 218). All the other directions about format (4–10) apply to both kinds of formal business letters.

68

4. **Flush** with the left-hand margin and in single-spaced block form, type the name and address of the person or the organization to whom the letter is written. (The same form will be used in addressing the envelope.) It is exceedingly important that the full name of the person to whom the letter is addressed be spelled correctly.

5. Two spaces below this inside address and flush with the left-hand margin, type the salutation, followed by a colon. In addressing an organization rather than a specific person in that organization, use salutations like **Dear Sir, Gentlemen, Dear Madam, Ladies.** If you know the name of the person in that organization, you should use the last name, prefaced with **Mr.** or **Miss** or **Mrs.** or **Ms.**, for example, **Dear Mr. Toler, Dear Miss Cameron, Dear Mrs. Nakamura, Dear Ms. Ingrao.** Women who feel that marital status should be no more specified in their own case than in that of a man (for whom **Mr.** serves, irrespective of whether he is married) prefer **Ms.** to **Mrs.** and **Miss.** The plural of **Mr.** is **Messrs.;** the plural of **Mrs.** or **Ms.** is **Mmes.;** the plural of **Miss** is **Misses.** Professional titles may also be used in the salutation: **Dear Professor Newman, Dear Dr. Martin.** (*Webster's New Collegiate Dictionary* carries an extensive list of the forms of address for various dignitaries—judges, clergy, legislators, etc.)

6. The body of the letter should be single-spaced, except for double-spacing between paragraphs. Paragraphs are not indented but start flush with the left-hand margin.

7. The usual complimentary closes for business letters are these: **Sincerely yours, Yours truly,** and **Very truly yours.** The complimentary close is followed by a comma.

8. Type your full name three or four spaces below the complimentary close. The typed name should not be prefaced with a professional title (**Dr., Rev.**) nor followed by a designation of academic degrees (**M.A., Ph.D.**), but below the typed name, you may indicate your official capacity (e.g., **Chair of the Board, Director of Personnel, Managing Editor**). You should sign your name in the space between the complimentary close and the typed name.

9. If copies of the letter are being sent to one or more others, that fact should be indicated with a notation like the following at the lower left-hand side of the page (**cc** is the abbreviation of **carbon copy**—a remnant of the days when copies were made on a typewriter with carbon paper):

68

cc. Mary Hunter
**   Robert Allison**

10. If the letter was dictated to, and typed by, a secretary, that fact should be indicated by a notation like the following, which is typed flush with the left-hand margin and below the writer's signature (the writer's initials are given in capital letters, the secretary's in lowercase letters): **WLT/cs** or **WLT:cs.**

    See the following models for the text and the envelope of the two styles of business letters.

69 Business Letter, Semiblock

239 Riverside Road
Columbus, OH 43210
January 5, 1996

Mr. Thomas J. Weiss
Manager, Survey Division
Acme Engineering Company, Inc.
Omaha, NE 68131

Dear Mr. Weiss:

Mr. Robert Miller, sales representative of the Rushmore
Caterpillar Company of Columbus and a longtime friend of my
father, told me that when he saw you at a convention in
Chicago recently, you indicated you would have two or three
temporary positions open this summer in your division. Mr.
Miller kindly offered to write you about me, but he urged
me to write also.

By June, I will have completed my junior year in the Department of Civil Engineering at Ohio State University. Not
only do I need to work this summer to finance my final year
of college, but I also need to get some practical experience in surveying tracts on a large road building project
such as your company is now engaged in. After checking
with several of the highway contractors in this area, I
have learned that all of them have already hired their
quota of engineering students for next summer.

For the last three summers, I have worked for the Worley
Building Contractors of Columbus as a carpenter's helper
and as a cement finisher. Mr. Albert Michaels, my foreman
for the last three summers, has indicated that he would
write a letter of reference for me, if you want one. He un-
derstands why I want to get some experience in surveying
this summer, but he told me that I would have priority for
a summertime job with Worley if I wanted it.

Among my instructors in civil engineering, the two men who
know me best are Dr. Theodore Sloan, who says that he knows
you, and Mr. A.M. Sister. Currently, I have a 3.2 quality-
point average in all my subjects, but I have straight A's
in all my engineering courses. For the last two quarters, I
have worked as a laboratory assistant for Professor Sloan.

I am anxious to get experience in my future profession, and
I am quite willing to establish temporary residence in
Omaha during the summer. I own a four-cylinder subcompact
car that I could use to travel to the job site each day. I
am in good health, and I would be available to work for
long hours and at odd hours during the summer months. If
you want any letters of recommendation from any of the men
named in my letter, please let me know.

cc. Robert Miller

Sincerely yours,

Oscar Jerman

Oscar Jerman

Business letter typed on plain, unlined paper.

70 Addressed Typed Business-size Envelope

Oscar Jerman
239 Riverside Road
Columbus, OH 43210

Mr. Thomas J. Weiss
Manager, Survey Division
Acme Engineering Company, Inc.
5868 Fanshawe Drive
Omaha, NB 68131

70

71 Business Letter, Full Block on Letterhead

Department of English

164 West 17th Avenue
Columbus, OH 43210-1370

Phone 614-292-6065
FAX   614-292-7816

July 1, 1996

Dr. Robert J. Myers, Executive Director
Association for Business Communication
Baruch College, CUNY
Speech Department
17 Lexington Avenue
New York, NY 10010

Dear Bob:

The enclosed disk contains the text and image files for the
ABC Web pages that are currently posted on Ohio State's
server. I've updated the list of officers to reflect the
results of our special election, changed the dues to reflect the Board of Directors' vote, and added information
about the 1997 regional conventions.

If the Baruch server supports forms, it would be a good
idea to set up an interactive membership form so that
people could join on-line. Of course, we'd need a secure
line so that people would feel comfortable giving their
credit card numbers.

When you have the pages posted on the Baruch server, let me
know, and I'll set up a "we've moved" link to the new address.

We should also send an announcement of the page to Netscape
and Mosaic so that they can include it on their "What's
New" lists and to Yahoo and several of the other search engines. Do you want to do that, or shall I?

Even though we've not yet announced our presence formally
to the Web, some people have found us: every now and then,
I get an e-mail from someone who has found our page and
wants more information. It will be good to have our pages
posted at ABC's Headquarters so that you can update them
regularly with current information about our conventions,
officers, and journals.

Sincerely,

Kitty O. Locker

Kitty O. Locker
Past President, Association for Business Communication

Business letter on letterhead stationery.

72 Addressed Letterhead Envelope

Department of English
164 West 17th Avenue
Columbus, OH 43210-1370

T · H · E
OHIO STATE
UNIVERSITY

Dr. Robert J. Myers, Executive Director
Association for Business Communication
Baruch College, CUNY
Speech Department
17 Lexington Avenue
New York, NY 10010

72

73 Two-Letter Postal Abbreviations

This is the U.S. Postal Service list of two-letter abbreviations of the fifty states, the District of Columbia, and outlying areas. These abbreviations should be set down in capital letters without a period and should be followed by the appropriate five- or nine-digit ZIP code, for example, 10022–5299.

73

Alabama	**AL**	Montana	**MT**
Alaska	**AK**	Nebraska	**NE**
Arizona	**AZ**	Nevada	**NV**
Arkansas	**AR**	New Hampshire	**NH**
California	**CA**	New Jersey	**NJ**
Colorado	**CO**	New Mexico	**NM**
Connecticut	**CT**	New York	**NY**
Delaware	**DE**	North Carolina	**NC**
District of Columbia	**DC**	North Dakota	**ND**
Florida	**FL**	Ohio	**OH**
Georgia	**GA**	Oklahoma	**OK**
Guam	**GU**	Oregon	**OR**
Hawaii	**HI**	Pennsylvania	**PA**
Idaho	**ID**	Puerto Rico	**PR**
Illinois	**IL**	Rhode Island	**RI**
Indiana	**IN**	South Carolina	**SC**
Iowa	**IA**	South Dakota	**SD**
Kansas	**KS**	Tennessee	**TN**
Kentucky	**KY**	Texas	**TX**
Louisiana	**LA**	Utah	**UT**
Maine	**ME**	Vermont	**VT**
Maryland	**MD**	Virginia	**VA**
Massachusetts	**MA**	Virgin Islands	**VI**
Michigan	**MI**	Washington	**WA**
Minnesota	**MN**	West Virginia	**WV**
Mississippi	**MS**	Wisconsin	**WI**
Missouri	**MO**	Wyoming	**WY**

Résumés

74 Résumé Writing

A résumé (pronounced *REZ-oo-may*) is also referred to, and sometimes even labeled with, the Latin terms *curriculum vitae* ("the course of one's life") or *vita brevis* ("a short life") or simply *vita*. Whatever name it bears, this document presents, usually on one or two pages and in the form of a list, a summary of an applicant's job objective, education, work experience, personal experiences, extracurricular activities, achievements, honors, and so on. Sent out with a cover letter that is addressed to a specific person in the company, the résumé is intended to introduce the applicant to a potential employer and to elicit a request for further information about the applicant and ultimately for an interview.

Under such headings as "Education," "Work Experience," and "Extracurricular Activities," the items are usually listed in reverse chronological order, starting with the most recent and ending with the earliest. The items that the applicant chooses to list should be pertinent to the kind of job being sought. The cover letter that accompanies the résumé should call attention to those items that are especially pertinent to the particular job that is being applied for.

The résumé and the cover letter should be neatly, flawlessly, and attractively typed on heavy bond paper. The physical appearance alone of these documents could make a crucial impression on the reader. You cannot afford to be sloppy or careless in preparing these documents. Remember that you are trying to sell yourself and the service you have to offer. So in listing your assets and achievements, do not misrepresent yourself, either by exaggerating or by downplaying your merits. Do not brag; let the facts speak for themselves.

For example, if you mention that you have a four-year grade-point average of 3.8, you do not have to boast that you have been an excellent student.

The résumé usually mentions that letters of reference and transcripts of academic work are available on request. In the case of students who are applying for a job, the résumé sometimes gives the address of the school's placement office, where the interested employer can write for the applicant's dossier, which is a collection of such documents as transcripts, letters of reference, and samples of one's writing. If your résumé and cover letter move the potential employer to write for your dossier, you will have reached an important stage in the process of applying for a job. The next important step is to gain an invitation to a face-to-face interview.

74

75 Résumé Format

```
                        MARY LEE HALE

          Home Address            Campus Address
          11 Top Street           45 Race Street
          Newark, OH 43055        Columbus, OH 43210
          (513) 267-4819          (614) 422-6866

JOB OBJECTIVE
   To obtain a job in an advertising or marketing capacity,
   with an emphasis on product development, sales, or promo-
   tional strategy.

EDUCATIONAL HIGHLIGHTS
   B.S. degree in Advertising, College of Communications,
   Ohio State University, Columbus, Ohio, 1996
   Equivalent of a minor in marketing
   Overall grade-point average: 3.4; major grade-point av-
   erage: 3.6

RELEVANT ADVERTISING AND MARKETING COURSES

   Introduction to Advertising            Advertising Media
   Creative Strategy and Tactics          Sales Writing
   Advertising in Contemporary Society    Marketing Research
   Advertising Management                 Marketing Behavior
   Advertising Research                   Operations Research

PRIOR WORK EXPERIENCE

Sept. 1995-  McBride's Pharmacy, Columbus, Ohio
present      Cashier

May-August   Industrial Techtonics, Weymouth, Ohio
1994         Market Development Coordinator
             --effected sales through personal calls
             --created a company brochure
             --gained new customers through correspondence

August 1994- Campus Daily News/Digest, Columbus, Ohio
March 1993   Advertising Manager and Sales Representative
             --conceived and executed advertising plans
             --maximized revenues by gaining new clients
             --motivated salespeople to become more efficient

August 1992- Rosalee Apparel, Inc., Columbus, Ohio
April 1990   Sales Clerk
             --introduced to the challenge of sales through
               commission system
             --developed the ability to relate to and meet
               the needs of a wide variety of people

EXTRACURRICULAR ACTIVITIES
   Dorm vice president     Skiing, tennis, needlepoint

References available on request
```

Glossary of Usage

Many of the entries here deal with pairs of words that writers often confuse because the words look or sound alike. Ascertain the distinction between these confusing pairs, and then invent your own memorizing device to help you make the right choice in a particular case. In all cases of disputed usage, the most conservative position on that usage is presented so that you can decide whether you want to run the risk of alienating that segment of your readers who subscribe to the conservative position on matters of language use.

accept, except. When writers don't keep their wits about them, they occasionally get these two words mixed up and inadvertently use the wrong word. Most of the time, **except** is used as a preposition, in the sense of "with the exclusion of, other than, but": *Everyone was dressed up except me.* The alternative prepositional form **excepting** should be used only in negative constructions: *Waiters must report all income to the IRS, not excepting tips.* Sometimes **except** is used as a conjunction, followed by **that**: *She would have called, except that she could not find his telephone number.* The word **accept** may never be used as a preposition—although in a careless moment, a writer might compose this sentence: *They approved of all the candidates accept him.* The word **accept** is a verb, in the sense of "to receive, to take in": *She graciously accepted his apology.* On the rare occasion when **except** is used as a verb, in the sense of "to exclude, to leave out, to omit," writers sometimes use the wrong verb, as in this sentence: *My brother was accepted from the dean's list because his grades were not high enough.* (Write instead, *My brother was excepted from the dean's list because his grades were not high enough.*) All in all, **accept** and **except** are tricky words. Be careful.

adverse, averse. Both of these words are adjectives that are used in the sense of opposition, but from different perspectives. The opposition expressed by the word **averse** is always from the subject's point of view, as in *The pastor was averse to their whispering in church* (that is, the pastor was opposed to their whispering in church). The opposition expressed by the word **adverse** exists outside the subject, as in *She overcame the adverse circumstances.* The idiomatic preposition to use with **averse** is **to.**

advice, advise. Adopt some mnemonic device to help you remember that **advice** is the noun form and that **advise** is the verb form: *She accepted his advice* (noun). *The doctors advised him to stop smoking* (verb). Pronouncing the two words may help you get the right spelling.

affect, effect. The noun form is almost always **effect** (*The effect of that usage was to alienate the purists*). The wrong choices are usually made when writers use the verb. The verb **effect** means "to bring about, to accomplish": *The prisoner effected his escape by picking a lock.* The verb **affect** means "to influence": *The weather affected her moods.*

allusion, illusion. Think of **allusion** as meaning "indirect reference": *He made an allusion to her parents.* Think of **illusion** as meaning "a deceptive impression": *He continued to entertain this illusion about her ancestry.*

alot, a lot. This locution should always be written as two words: *A lot of the natives lost faith in the government.*

already, all ready. **All ready** is an adjective phrase meaning "completely prepared": *By 3:00, the team was all ready to go.* **Already** is an adverb, meaning "by this time, previously": *By 3:00, the team had already left the gymnasium.*

alright, allright, all right. **All right** is the only correct way to write this expression: *He told his mother that he was all right.*

altogether, all together. Altogether is the adverb form, in the sense of "completely": *She was not altogether happy with the present.* **All together** is an adjective phrase, in the sense of "unified": *The students were all together in their loyalty to the team.*

among. See **between.**

amount of, number of. When you are speaking of masses or bulks, use **amount of:** *They bought a large amount of sugar.* When you are speaking of persons or things that can be counted one by one, use **number of:** *They bought a large number of cookies.* See **fewer, less.**

any more. The adverb phrase **any more** should not be used in positive statements, as in these instances: *They were surprised that you visit us any more* and *The television stations have good programs any more.* But this adverb may be used in negative statements, as in the following instances: *They were surprised that you do not visit us any more* and *The television stations don't have good programs any more;* and in questions, as in this instance: *Do you write to your parents any more?* Most arbiters of usage recommend that this adverb be written as two words, but at least two of the reputable dictionaries authorize the single-word form, **anymore.**

as, like. See **like, as.**

because of. See **due to.**

beside, besides. Both of these words are used as prepositions, but **beside** means "at the side of": *They built a cabin beside a lake.* **Besides** means "in addition to": *They bought a jacket besides a pair of boots.*

between. The conservative position is that **between** should be used only when two persons or things are involved: *They made a choice between the Democrat and the Republican.* Use **among** when three or more persons or things are involved: *Faced with a half dozen choices, he could not decide among them.*

can't help but. Conservatives regard this expression as an instance of double negatives (**can't** and **but**). This sentence, *She can't help but love him,* they would rewrite as *She can't help loving him.*

center around. One frequently sees and hears an expression such as *His interest centered around his work.* This expression seems to violate the basic metaphor from which it derives: How can something center **around** something else? Say instead, *His interest centered* **on** *his work* or *His interest centered* **upon** *his work.*

complement, compliment. Writers frequently mix up these like-sounding words. **Complement,** both as a noun and as a verb, carries the notion of "something that completes or adds to": *Traveling complements the education we get in school.* **Compliment,** both as a noun and as a verb, carries the notion of "an expression of praise": *He grinned from ear to ear whenever his teacher paid him a compliment.* Devise your own mnemonic device to help you write the right word for what you intend to say.

comprise. Comprise is a tricky word. This verb means "to include," so it is correct to write *This state comprises seventeen counties.* It is incorrect to write *Seventeen counties comprise the state* or *The state is comprised of seventeen counties.* The formula is "The whole comprises the parts. The parts do not comprise the whole." Instead of saying *The state is comprised of seventeen counties,* say *The state is composed of seventeen counties.* Be wary of this tricky word.

continual, continuous. There is a real distinction between these two adjectives. Think of **continual** as referring to something that occurs repeatedly (that is, with interruptions). For instance, a noise that recurred every three or four minutes would be a "continual noise"; a noise that persisted without interruptions for an hour would be a "continuous noise." **Continual** is stop-and-go; **continuous** is an uninterrupted flow.

could of, should of, would of, may of, might of. In the spoken language, these forms sound very much like the correct forms. In writing, use the correct forms: **could have, should have, would have, may have, might have.** In informal contexts, you may use the accepted contractions, such as **could've, should've, would've.**

data. The word **data,** like the words **criteria, phenomena,** and **media,** is a plural noun and therefore demands the plural form of the demonstrative adjective (*these data, those data*) and the plural form of the verb: *These data present convincing evidence of his guilt. The data were submitted by the committee.*

different from, different than. In British usage, **different than** may be used when a clause follows the expression: *This treatment is different than we expected.* In conservative American usage, **different from** is preferred to **different than,** whether the expression is followed by a noun phrase (*The British usage is different from the American usage*) or by a noun clause (*This treatment is different from what we expected*).

disinterested, uninterested. Careful writers still make a distinction between these two words. For them, **disinterested** means "unbiased, impartial, objective": *The mother could not make a disinterested judgment about her son.* **Uninterested,** for them, means "bored, indifferent to": *The students were obviously uninterested in the lecture.*

due to, because of. Many writers use **due to** and **because of** interchangeably. Some writers, however, observe the conservative distinction between these two expressions: **due to** is an adjectival construction, and **because of** is an adverbial construction. Accordingly, they would always follow any form of the verb **to be** (**is, were, has been,** etc.) with **due to:** *His absence last week was due to illness.* They would always follow transitive and intransitive verbs with the adverbial construction **because of:** *She missed the party because of illness* and *He failed because of illness.* Sometimes, they might substitute **owing to** or **on account of** for **because of.**

effect. See **affect.**

enthuse, enthused. You will frequently hear these used as verbs, as in the sentence *They enthused about the plans for the dance.* Linguists would call this verb form a *back formation* from the noun **enthusiasm** or the adjective **enthusiastic.** Purists frown on this verb form. They would say *They were enthusiastic about the plans for the dance.*

farther, further. Conservatives insist that **farther** is the correct word to use when one is referring to physical distance, as in the sentence *The campers traveled farther than they expected on that day.* They insist that **further** is the correct word to use in the figurative or abstract sense of additional time, degree, or quantity, as in sentences such as these: *The campers took off without further delay, The teacher insisted that they consider the matter further,* and *They demanded a further explanation for the delay.* Although no one ever uses **farther** in the abstract or figurative sense (for instance, *They gave the matter farther consideration*), some writers will use **further** where conservatives insist on the use of **farther** (for instance, *That mountain is further away than I thought*). Observe the traditional distinction between **farther** and **further** if you do not want to run the risk of alienating some of your readers.

fewer, less. Use **fewer** with countable items: *That beer has fewer calories in it than the Canadian beer has.* Use **less** when speaking of mass or bulk: *Elmer has less sand in his garden than Andrew does.* See **amount of, number of.**

good, well. If you remember that **good** is an adjective and that **well** is an adverb, you won't write *He did good on the exam* or *The car runs good.* Instead, you will write *He did well on the exam* and *The car runs well.* And you will write *She is good about taking her medicine* and *The pie tastes good.*

hopefully. Many people object to the use of **hopefully** in the sense of "it is to be hoped," as in the sentence *Hopefully, we can finish our term papers by the deadline.* If you want to avoid offending those who object to this usage, you will rewrite a sentence like the one above to read *We hope that we can finish our term papers by the deadline.*

human, humans. Those who take a conservative view of language have not yet accepted **human** or **humans** as a noun. They would rewrite *The natives made no distinction between animals and humans* in this fashion: *The natives made no distinction between animals and human beings.* In their view, **human** should be used only as an adjective.

imply, infer. There is a definite difference in meaning between these two verbs. **Imply** means "to hint at, to suggest," as in *She implied that she wouldn't come to his party.* **Infer** means "to deduce, to draw a conclusion from," as in *He inferred from the look on her face that she wouldn't come to the party.*

irregardless. This is one of the "double negatives" (**ir-** and **-less**) that in some people's minds does irreparable damage to the user's reputation as a literate person. If you use the word **regardless,** your reputation for irreproachable literacy will be preserved.

kind of, sort of. Do not use the article **a** or **an** with either of these phrases: *He suffered some kind of a heart attack* and *She got the sort of an ovation that she deserved.* Rewrite these sentences in this way: *He suffered some kind of heart attack* and *She got the sort of ovation that she deserved.* **Kind of** and **sort of** in the sense of "rather" or "somewhat" (*He was kind of annoyed at his teacher*) should be reserved for an informal or a colloquial context.

lend, loan. The conservative position is that **loan** should be used exclusively as a noun (*He took out a loan from the bank*) and that **lend** should be used exclusively as a verb (*The bank will lend him the down payment*).

less. See **fewer.**

lie, lay. Lie (past tense **lay,** present participle **lying,** past participle **lain**) is an intransitive verb meaning "to rest, to recline," as in *The* *book is lying on the table, The book lay there yesterday,* and *It has lain there for three days.* **Lay** (past tense **laid,** present participle **laying,** past participle **laid**) is a transitive verb (that is, it must be followed by an object) meaning "to put down," as in *She is laying the book on the table* and *Yesterday, she laid the book on the mantelpiece.*

like, as. Avoid the use of **like** as a subordinating conjunction, as in *At the party, he behaves like he does in church.* Use **like** exclusively as a preposition: *At a party, he behaves like a prude.* **As** is the appropriate subordinating conjunction with clauses: *At a party, he behaves as he does in church.*

likely, liable, apt. Some writers use these words interchangeably: *Their daughter is likely* (or *liable* or *apt*) *to get her way.* Discriminating writers, however, reserve **liable** for an undesirable happening, as in *If he is contradicted, he is liable to lose his temper,* and reserve **likely** for a favorable happening, as in *If he is contradicted, he is likely to smile and shake your hand warmly.* **Liable** is also the word to use in legal contexts, as in *If you don't remove the snow from your sidewalk, you are liable to be fined.* **Apt** is used in the sense of "inclined," as in *It is apt to be foggy here early in the morning,* and also in the sense of "appropriate or suitable," as in *That was an apt remark.*

literally. Originally, **literally** was used as an adverb meaning the opposite of **figuratively.** In recent years, some people have been using the word as an intensifier: *She literally blew her top.* Careful writers still use the word in its original sense of "actually": *The mother literally washed out her son's mouth with soap after his outburst of profanity.*

loose, lose. These common words look alike but do not sound alike, and they differ in meaning (**loose,** "unfastened"; **lose,** "mislay"). Here is a device to help you remember the difference in meaning. The two *o*'s in **loose** are like marbles dumped out of a can: *The dog broke its leash and ran loose in the backyard.* The word **lose** has lost one of its *o*'s: *I always lose my wallet whenever I go to a carnival.* If this mnemonic device does not help you keep the two words straight, invent your own device.

may of, might of. See **could of.**

off of. *My youngest son skinned his nose when he jumped off of the moving carousel.* Using **of** with **off,** as in the previous sentence, is redundant. Say simply *He jumped off the moving carousel.*

OK This most distinctively American expression has appeared in various forms in the written medium: **O.K., okay, oke, okeh,** and **okey,** among others. But **OK** is the prevailing form. This versatile word has been used as a noun *(My boss gave his OK to my plan);* as a verb *(The directors OK the project);* as an adjective *(That was an OK thing to do* or *He said it was OK for me to leave the door unlocked);* as an adverb *(The computer was working OK when I left it);* and as an interjection *(OK, so let's get going).* There is widespread agreement among the arbiters of usage that **OK** is acceptable in informal, colloquial contexts. **OK** is widely used in written communications in the business world.

past, passed. These words are more sound-alikes than look-alikes. The word with the *-ed* ending is the only one that can be used as a verb: *His car passed mine on the freeway.* The word **past** is versatile: it can be used as a noun *(I recalled my sordid past);* as an adjective *(I recalled the past events);* and as a preposition *(His car sped past mine like a bullet).* But **past** should never be used as a verb, as in this sentence: *His car past mine.*

principal, principle. These words sound alike, but they are spelled differently, and they have different meanings. Whether used as a noun or as an adjective, **principal** carries the meaning of "chief." The noun form to designate the chief of a high school is **principal.** (Some people use this mnemonic device to guide them in using the right spelling for the chief officer of a high school: "The **principal** is your **pal.**") The adjective that means "chief" is always **principal:** *The principal administrative officer of a high school is the principal.* The word

principle is used only as a noun and means "rule, law": *A manufacturer should observe the basic principles of physics.*

quote(s). In formal contexts, use **quotation(s)** instead of the colloquial contraction **quote(s).**

reason is because. This phrasing constitutes an example of faulty predication. Write *The reason is that* . . .

reason why. This phrasing is redundant. A reason is a *why*. Instead of writing *The reason why I am unhappy is that I lost my wallet,* drop the redundant **why** and write *The reason I am unhappy is that I lost my wallet.*

respectfully, respectively. Choose the correct adverb for what you want to say. **Respectfully** means "with respect": *She answered the questions very respectfully.* **Respectively** means "the previously mentioned items in the order in which they are listed": *Mary Sarton, Maria Gonzalez, and Sarah Fowler were the first, second, and third presidents of the guild, respectively.*

set, sit. Set, like **lay,** is a transitive verb (that is, it takes an object, as in *She set the vase down carefully on the table*). **Sit,** like **lie,** is an intransitive verb (that is, it expresses action but action that does not terminate in an object). So you should write *They sit on the porch,* not *They set on the porch.* However, there are a few idioms in which **set** is used as an intransitive verb: *The sun sets* and *A hen sets.* And there are at least two idioms in which **sit** is used as a transitive verb: *She sits herself down* and *A rider sits a horse.*

should of. See **could of.**

so, such. Avoid the use of **so** or **such** as an intensifier, as in sentences such as *She was so happy* and *It was such a cold day.* If you must use an intensifier, use such adverbs as **very, exceedingly,** and **unusually:** *She was very happy* and *It was an unusually cold day.* If you use **so** and **such** to modify an adjective, your readers have a right to expect you to complete the structure with a *that* clause of result: *She was so happy that she clapped her hands for a full two minutes* and *It was so cold that we had to clap our hands to keep warm.*

sort of. See **kind of.**

supposed to, used to. Because it is difficult to hear the *-d* when these phrases are spoken, writers sometimes write *He was suppose to arrive yesterday* or *He use to eat here at noon.* Always add the letter *-d* to these words.

their, there, they're. These are probably the commonest homonyms in the English language; that is, words that are spelled differently but that are pronounced alike. The wrong word is chosen in a particular instance not because the writer does not know better but because the writer has been careless or inattentive. (Is there any of us who has not occasionally used the wrong one of these three words when we were writing?) Because every literate person knows the different meanings of these three words, we do not have to review those meanings here. Just be careful to use the right word for what you want to say.

try and. In the spoken medium, one frequently hears utterances such as *Try and stay within the white lines if you can.* Purists insist that we write *Try to stay within the white lines if you can.* So if you want to be "proper," you should always write **try to** instead of **try and.**

unique. The word **unique** basically means "one of a kind." Purists, therefore, insist that it is just as ridiculous to say *more unique* or *most unique* as it is to say *more perfect* or *most perfect.* It is highly likely that such qualifications of the word **unique** will eventually be acceptable, if they are not already sanctioned by most arbiters of usage. But if you do not want to raise the eyebrows of any of your readers, do not write such sentences as *Their policy is the most unique one in the industry.* What is not debatable is that the article **a**, not **an**, should be used in front of **unique**: *That is a unique policy.*

used to. See **supposed to.**

whose, who's. Since these two words are pronounced alike, it is understandable that writers sometimes make the wrong choice. The word spelled with the apostrophe is the contraction of *who is: Who's the principal actor? Who's playing the lead role?* **Whose** is (1) the interrogative of the pronoun **who** *(Whose hat is this?)*; (2) the possessive case of the relative pronoun **who** *(John is the man whose son died last week)*, and (3) an acceptable possessive form of the relative pronoun **which** *(Our flag, whose broad stripes and bright stars we watched through the perilous fight, was gallantly streaming over the ramparts).*

would of. See **could of.**

you. **You** is the second-person personal pronoun, both singular and plural. We all recognize when this pronoun is referring to a definite person, as in *My dear, I am asking you if you will marry me,* or to definite persons, as in *I ask all of you to give me your undivided attention.* What has become questionable usage is the use of the indefinite **you,** as in *Today, you have to be rich in order to survive* and *Most doctors agree that if you avoid fatty foods, you will lessen the chance of your having a heart attack.* In those sentences, the **you** is not a real person out there. In those sentences, **you** is being used where careful writers use the indefinite pronoun **one,** as in *Today, one has to be rich in order to survive.* Each writer has to decide whether he or she will adopt the increasingly prevalent practice of using the indefinite **you.**

Glossary of Grammatical Terms

Although the entries contained in this glossary of grammatical terms are useful to all students of writing, the entries preceded by underlined words or phrases are probably most useful to those whose native language is not English.

active verb. See **passive verb.**

adjective clause. An adjective clause is a dependent clause that modifies a noun or pronoun, much as a simple adjective does.

The relative pronouns *who, which,* and *that* often appear at the beginning of the adjective clause, serving as the connecting link between the modified noun or pronoun and the clause that follows.

The car, **which was old and battered,** served us well.

Those are the houses **that I love best.**

Sometimes, the relative pronoun is unexpressed but understood:

The book **I was reading** held my attention. (Here **that** is understood: The book **that** I was reading.)

See **dependent clause, modifier, nonrestrictive adjective clause, relative pronoun, restrictive adjective clause.**

adverb clause. An adverb clause is a dependent clause that modifies a verb or verbal, much as a simple adverb does.

The subordinating conjunction (**when, because, so that,** etc.) that appears at the head of the clause links the adverb clause to the word that it modifies.

When I was ready, I took the examination.

I took the examination **because I was ready.**

To take the examination **when you are not ready** is dangerous. (Here the adverb clause modifies the infinitive **to take.**)

The verb after the subordinating conjunction in an adverb clause of time is never in the future even though the sentence is about the future. Note the following example:

Incorrect: When I will finish class, I will do the laundry.

Rewrite: When I finish class, I will do the laundry.

Avoid adding unnecessary connectors after an adverb clause. In the example below, **although** expresses the idea of contrast; **but** is not necessary here.

Incorrect: Although the test was difficult, but I got an A.

Rewrite: Although the test was difficult, I got an A.

See **dependent clause, modifier, subordinating conjunction, verbal.**

antecedent. An antecedent is the noun that a pronoun refers to or "stands for."

In the previous sentence, for example, the antecedent of the relative pronoun **that** is **noun.** In the sentence *The mother told her son that his check had arrived,* **mother** is the antecedent of the pronoun **her,** and **son** is the antecedent of the pronoun **his.**

See **relative pronoun.**

<u>articles.</u> Indefinite articles **(a/an)** precede singular count nouns that are not previously specified (*I need* **a new car.**) All singular count nouns need an article or an equivalent:

Incorrect: He became ☀ teacher in 1988.

Rewrite: He became a teacher in 1988.

The **definite article (the)** has many uses. Use **the** before a count or noncount noun that has been previously specified: *I'm buying a house. The house is white, with green trim.* Use **the** before a count or noncount noun that has been modified: **the** books that I read; **the** movie about dinosaurs. Use **the** after quantity terms: all of **the** students; most of **the** cheese. Don't use **the** to make generalizations with abstract nouns:

Incorrect: The pollution is a major problem in Los Angeles.

Rewrite: Pollution is a major problem in Los Angeles.

Note the errors in the following sentences:

Incorrect: All of ⊛ students failed the exam.

Rewrite: All of **the** students failed the exam.

Incorrect: I returned to ⊛ village where I grew up.

Rewrite: I returned to **the** village where I grew up.

auxiliary verbs. Auxiliary verbs are those function words—"helping" words (hence *auxiliary*)—that accompany other verb forms to indicate tense or mood or voice.

The words in boldface are auxiliary verbs:

She **will** walk to work. She **is** walking to work. She **has** walked to work.
She **has been** walking to work. She **could** walk to work. She **must** walk to work.
She **was** driven to work.

Some verbs in English require no auxiliary verb (e.g., *I work*), while others require one or more (e.g., *I should have been given a raise*). Watch for these common problems when writing sentences with one or more auxiliary verbs.

Use the past participle (verb ending in *-ed*) after the auxiliaries **have, has,** and **had.**

Incorrect: She **has walking** to work.

Rewrite: She **has walked** to work.

Incorrect: She **has being** here for one week.

Rewrite: She **has been** here for one week.

Add the appropriate form of the auxiliary verb **be** before the verb form ending in *-ing:*

Incorrect: She walking right now.

Rewrite: She **is** walking right now.

The following sentences are passive; the auxiliary **be** is followed by the past participal (verb ending in *-ed*):

Incorrect: She **was been** given a raise.

Rewrite: She **was** given a raise.

or

She **has been** given a raise.

When preceded by an auxiliary verb, the main verb may have one of three forms, as follows:

1. The **stem form** of the verb comes after **will** and modal auxiliaries such as **can, could, may, might, would, must,** and **have to.**

   She will **work.**
   They can **drive.**

2. The **past participle** (verb form ending in *-ed*) comes after the auxiliary **be** in passive sentences and after **have, has, had** in active sentences:

I was **elected** president of the class. **(passive sentence)**
He had **written** the book in 1993. **(active sentence)**

3. Use the *-ing* form of the verb after the auxiliary **be** in active sentences:

She is **leaving**.
She will be **leaving**.
She has been **talking**.

See **modal auxiliary, verb tense, voice.**

clause. See **dependent clause, independent clause.**

comma splice. A comma splice is the use of a comma, instead of a coordinating conjunction or a semicolon, between the two independent clauses of a compound sentence.

Incorrect: He could not tolerate noise, noise made him nervous and irritable.

Rewrite: He could not tolerate noise, for noise made him nervous and irritable.

Since the comma is a separating device rather than a joining device, it must be accompanied in this sentence by a coordinating conjunction (here **for**), or it must be replaced with a semicolon.

See **compound sentence, coordinating conjunction, independent clause.**

complement. A complement is the word or phrase, following a verb, that "completes" the predicate of a clause.

A complement may be (1) the object of a transitive verb (He hit **the ball**); (2) the noun or noun phrase following the verb **to be** (He is **an honors student**), or (3) the adjective following the verb **to be** or a linking verb (He is **happy**. The milk tastes **sour**).

See **linking verb, noun phrase, predicate complement, transitive verb, to be.**

complex sentence. A complex sentence is one that consists of one independent clause and one or more dependent clauses.

The following complex sentence has in addition to an independent clause two dependent clauses—the first one an adverb clause, the second an adjective clause.

> **When she got to the microphone,** she made a proposal **that won unanimous approval.**

As used by grammarians, the term has nothing to do with the length or complexity of the sentence.

See **dependent clause, independent clause.**

compound sentence. A compound sentence is one that consists of two or more independent clauses.

> He was twenty-one, but she was only eighteen.
> Young men are idealists; old men are realists.

See **comma splice, independent clause.**

conjunctive adverb. A conjunctive adverb is a word or phrase that links parts of sentences logically. Some of the common conjunctive adverbs are **however, therefore, nevertheless, moreover, instead, furthermore, consequently, meanwhile, in the meantime, for example, on the contrary, as a result,** and **in addition.**

On the contrary and **in contrast** do not have the same meaning:

> This exercise is quite easy; the other, **in contrast,** is extremely difficult.

(**In contrast** shows how two, usually different, things or situations are contrasting.)

> He isn't a poor student; **on the contrary,** he got the highest grade in the class.

(**On the contrary** is an expression of emphasis. In this latter sentence, the idea in the first clause is reinforced, not contrasted, by the second clause.)

coordinate. Words, phrases, and clauses of the same grammatical kind or of equal rank are said to be coordinate.

A pair or series of nouns, for instance, would be a coordinate unit. An infinitive phrase yoked with a participial phrase would not be a coordinate unit and should not be joined, because the phrases are not of the same grammatical kind. An independent clause would not be coordinate with a dependent or subordinate clause, because the two clauses are not of equal rank. An alternative term for **coordinate** is **parallel**.

See **coordinating conjunction, parallelism.**

coordinating conjunction. A coordinating conjunction is a word that joins words, phrases, or clauses of the same kind or rank. It joins nouns with nouns, verbs with verbs, prepositional phrases with prepositional phrases, independent clauses with independent clauses, adverb clauses with adverb clauses, and so on.

A coordinating conjunction cannot be used to join a noun with an adjective, a prepositional phrase with a gerund phrase, or an independent clause with a dependent clause.

The coordinating conjunctions are **and, but, or, for, nor, yet, so.**

Note the meanings of these two coordinating conjunctions: **for** and **yet**.

> She returned to school, **for** she wants to be a nurse. (Use **for** to express the cause of, or the reason for, something.)
>
> They did not speak the same language, **yet** they became friends. (Use **yet** to express a contrasting or surprising idea; it is a synonym for **but**.)

Place the comma *before* the coordinating conjunction:

Incorrect: She returned to school for, she wants to be a nurse.

Rewrite: She returned to school, for she wants to be a nurse.

correlative conjunctions. Correlative conjunctions are coordinating conjunctions that operate in pairs to join coordinate structures in a sentence.

The common correlative conjunctions are **either . . . or, neither . . . nor, both . . . and, not only . . . but also,** and **whether . . . or.**

By this act, she renounced **both** her citizenship **and** her civil rights.

Use inverted (question) word order after **not only** and **neither . . . nor** as follows:

Incorrect: Not only he wants a raise, but he also wants additional vacation time.

Rewrite: Not only **does he want** a raise, but he also wants additional vacation time.

Incorrect: Neither he will resign, nor I will ask him to.

Rewrite: Neither **will he resign, nor will I ask** him to.

See **coordinate, coordinating conjunction.**

count noun. See **nouns, count and noncount.**

dangling verbal. A dangling verbal is a participle, gerund, or infinitive (or a phrase formed with one of these verbals) that is either unattached to a noun or pronoun or attached to the wrong noun or pronoun:

Incorrect: Raising his glass, a toast was proposed to the newlyweds by the bride's father.

Rewrite: Raising his glass, the bride's father proposed a toast to the newlyweds.

In this sentence, the participial phrase **raising his glass** is attached to the wrong noun (**toast**) and therefore is said to be "dangling" (it was not the **toast** that was doing the **raising**). The participial phrase will be properly attached if the noun **father** is made the subject of the sentence.

See **verbal, verbal phrase.**

dependent clause. A dependent clause is a group of words that has a subject and a predicate made up of a finite verb but that is made part of, or dependent on, a larger structure by a relative pronoun (**who, which, that**) or by a subordinating conjunction (**when, if, because, although,** etc.).

There are three kinds of dependent clauses: the *adjective clause,* the *adverb clause,* and the *noun clause.*

A **dependent clause** cannot stand by itself; it must be joined to an **independent clause** that makes it part of a complete sentence. A dependent clause written with an initial capital letter and with a period or question mark at the end is one of the structures that are called **sentence fragments.** An alternative term for **dependent clause** is **subordinate clause.**

See **adjective clause, adverb clause, finite verb, independent clause, noun clause, subordinating conjunction.**

faulty predication. A faulty predication occurs when the verb or verb phrase of a clause does not fit semantically or syntactically with the subject or noun phrase of the clause. It results from the choice of incompatible words or structures:

> **Incorrect:** The reason I couldn't go was **because I hadn't completed my homework.**

> **Rewrite:** The reason I couldn't go was **that I hadn't completed my homework.**

The verb **claimed** in the first sentence above is semantically incompatible with the noun phrase **the shortage of funds,** which serves as the subject of the clause. In the second sentence, the adverbial **because** clause is incompatible as a predicate complement following the verb **was.** The noun clause **that I hadn't completed my homework** is syntactically compatible as a predicate complement for the verb *was.*

See **noun clause, predicate complement, predicate verb, semantics, syntax, verb phrase.**

finite verb. A finite verb is a verb that is fixed or limited, by its form, in person, number, and tense.

In the sentence "The boy runs to school," the verb **runs** is fixed by its form in person (cf. **I run, you run**), in number (cf. **They run**), and in tense (cf. **he ran**). The verbals (participle, gerund, infinitive) are considered **infinite verbs** because although they are fixed in their form in regard to tense (present and past), they are not limited in person or number. The minimal units of a clause, whether it is dependent or independent, are a subject (a noun or pronoun, a noun phrase, or a noun clause) and a finite verb:

Bells ring. (but not: **Bells ringing.**)

See **noun phrase, predicate verb, verbal.**

fused sentence. A **fused sentence,** which is a serious error, is the joining of two or more independent clauses without any punctuation or coordinating conjunction between them:

She could not believe her eyes mangled bodies were strewn all over the highway.

Correct this fused sentence by putting a period after *eyes* and capitalizing *mangled*. A fused sentence is also called a **run-on sentence** or a **run-together sentence.**

See **comma splice, independent clause.**

gerund. A gerund, one of the verbals, is a word that is formed from a verb but that functions as a noun.

Because of its hybrid nature as part verb and part noun, a gerund may take an object, may be modified by an adverb, and may serve in a sentence any function that a noun can perform. Since, like the present participle, it is formed by adding *-ing* to the base verb, one can distinguish the gerund from the participle by noting whether it functions in the sentence as a noun rather than as an adjective. The following are examples of the gerund or gerund phrase performing various functions of the noun:

As the subject of the sentence: Hiking is his favorite exercise.
As the object of a verb: He favored **raising the funds by subscription.**
As the complement of the verb to be: His most difficult task was **reading all the fine print.**
As the object of a preposition: After **reading the book,** he took the examination.

The latter sentence would be considered a dangling verbal if it were phrased as follows:

After reading the book, the examination had to be taken.

See **dangling verbal, verbal phrase.**

independent clause. An independent clause is a group of words that has a subject and a finite verb and that is not made part of a larger structure by a relative pronoun or a subordinating conjunction.

The following group of words is an independent clause because it has a subject and a finite verb:

The **girls tossed** the ball.

The following group of words has the same subject and finite verb, but it is not an independent clause because it is made part of a larger structure by the subordinating conjunction **when:**

When the girls tossed the ball.

The **when** turns the clause into an adverb clause and thereby makes it part of a larger structure: a sentence consisting of a dependent clause (the adverb clause) and an independent clause (**which** must be supplied here to make a complete sentence).

See **dependent clause, finite verb, relative pronoun, subordinating conjunction.**

infinitive. An infinitive is a word that is formed from a verb but that functions in the sentence as a noun or as an adjective or as an adverb.

Capable of functioning in these ways, the infinitive is more versatile than the participle, which functions only as an adjective, or the gerund, which functions only as a noun. The infinitive is formed by putting **to** in front of the base form of the verb.

Here are some examples of the infinitive or infinitive phrase in its various functions:

As a noun (subject of a sentence): To err is human; **to forgive** is divine.
As an adjective (modifying a noun—in this case, place): He wanted a place **to store his furniture.**
As an adverb (modifying a verb—in this case, waved): She waved a handkerchief **to gain his attention.**

The infinitive phrase in the following sentence would be considered a dangling verbal:

Incorrect: To prevent infection, the finger should be thoroughly washed.

Rewrite: To prevent infection, you should wash the finger thoroughly.

See **dangling verbal, verbal phrase.**

infinitives versus **gerunds.** Students of English as a second language (ESL) may have difficulty deciding whether to use a gerund or an infinitive form of a verb. Consider the errors in the following sentences:

Incorrect: She avoided **to go** to the dentist.

Rewrite: She avoided **going** to the dentist.

The verb **avoid** is followed by a gerund (**going**) and not an infinitive (**to go**). Other verbs that must be followed by a gerund are **admit, appreciate, can't help, delay, discuss, dislike, enjoy, finish, give up, help, imagine, miss, postpone, practice, risk, suggest,** and **tolerate.**

Incorrect: He refused **going** with me.

Rewrite: He refused **to go** with me.

The verb **refuse** is followed by an infinitive. Other common verbs that must be followed by an infinitive are **hope, want, expect, need, decide, plan, choose, claim, fail, pretend, bother,** and **manage.**

Incorrect: She was interested **to go.**

Rewrite: She was interested in **going.**

Incorrect: I'm looking forward **to go** with you.

Rewrite: I'm looking forward to **going** with you.

A gerund must follow all prepositions in English. In the first sentence, the preposition is **in.** In the second sentence, **to** is a preposition; it is not part of an infinitive, so it must be followed by the gerund **going.**

Incorrect: My parents let me **to go** on my own.

Rewrite: My parents let me **go** on my own.

Some verbs (e.g., **let, make,** and **have**) are followed by the stem form (the infinitive without **to**) of the verb.

It should be pointed out that in this section—and in several other sections of this glossary—we are dealing not so much with grammar or style as with the idiom of the English language.

intransitive verb. An intransitive verb is a verb that expresses action but that does not take an object.

Intransitive verbs cannot be used in the passive voice. Most action verbs in English have both transitive and intransitive uses, like **I ran swiftly** (intransitive) and **I ran a good race** (transitive). But some verbs can be used only transitively, like the verb **to emit,** and some verbs can be used only intransitively, like the verb **to go.** If in doubt about whether a particular verb can be used both transitively and intransitively, consult a dictionary.

The following verbs are all used intransitively:

He **swam** effortlessly.
They **slept** for twelve hours.
She **quarreled** with her neighbors.

See **passive verb, transitive verb, voice.**

linking verb. Linking verbs are verbs of the senses, like **feel, look, smell, taste,** and **sound,** and a limited number of other verbs, like **seem, remain, become,** and **appear,** that "link" the subject of the sentence with a complement.

Linking verbs are followed by an adjective or a noun or a noun phrase that serves as the complement:

The sweater **felt** soft. **(Adjective as complement)**
He **appeared** calm. **(Adjective as complement)**
She **remains** the president of the union. **(Noun phrase as complement)**

See **complement, noun phrase, predicate complement, to be.**

modal auxiliaries. These are a special type of auxiliary verb used to express an attitude about a situation (e.g., politeness: **Could** you help me? necessity: You **must** pay your bills; advice: You **should** lose some weight; possibility: It **might** rain tomorrow). Modal auxiliaries are usually followed by the stem of the verb, as in the examples above, but the past participle (form of the verb ending in -*ed*) follows perfect-tense modals (e.g., I should have **worked** later).

Here are some common errors to avoid when using modal auxiliaries:

Incorrect: We can't **to leave** until the storm passes.

Rewrite: We can't **leave** until the storm passes.

Use the past participle (e.g., **been**) after perfect-tense modals (e.g., **should have**):

Incorrect: The professor should have **being** more understanding of our language problems.

Rewrite: The professor should have **been** more understanding of our language problems.

modifier. A modifier is a word, phrase, or clause that limits, specifies, or describes another word.

In the phrase *the red barn,* the adjectival modifier **red** helps to specify or describe the particular barn being talked about. In the phrase *ran swiftly,* the adverbial modifier **swiftly** describes the manner in which the action designated by the verb **ran** was done. Phrases and clauses also modify nouns and verbs:

the girl **with the flowery hat** (Prepositional phrase modifying **girl**)
the barn **that is painted red** (Adjective clause modifying **barn**)
He ran **down the street.** (Prepositional phrase modifying **ran**)
He ran **because he was frightened.** (Adverb clause modifying **ran**)

Besides modifying verbs, adverbs also modify adjectives and other adverbs:

It was an **unusually** brilliant color. (Modifying the adjective **brilliant**)
He ran **very** swiftly. (Modifying the adverb **swiftly**)

See **adjective clause, adverb clause.**

nonrestrictive adjective clause. A nonrestrictive adjective clause is a dependent clause that supplies information about the noun or pronoun that it modifies, but information that is not needed to identify or specify the particular noun or pronoun being talked about:

My father, **who is a college graduate,** cannot get a job.

In this sentence, the adjective clause **who is a college graduate** supplies information about the father, but that information is not needed to identify which father is being talked about. The particular father being talked about is sufficiently identified by **my.**

A nonrestrictive adjective clause must be separated with a comma from the noun or pronoun that it modifies and is followed by another comma when the clause does not occur at the end of a sentence.

See **adjective clause, modifier, restrictive adjective clause.**

noun clause. A noun clause is a dependent clause that can serve almost every function that a noun or pronoun or noun phrase can serve: as the subject of the sentence, as an appositive to a noun, as the complement of a verb, or as the object of a preposition, but not as an indirect object.

The subordinating conjunctions that most often introduce a noun clause are **that** and **whether,** although **that** is sometimes omitted when the noun clause serves as the object of a transitive verb. (And, incidentally, the conjunction **that** differs from the relative pronoun **that,** which commonly introduces restrictive adjective clauses.)

That she would pass the course was evident to everyone. **(Subject of sentence)**

He said **he would not come. (Object of verb; that** is omitted here, but it is just as correct to say **that he would not come)**

The fact **that I had been sick** did not influence their decision. (In apposition to **fact)**

They asked me about **whether I had seen him recently.** (Object of the preposition **about)**

See **complement, dependent clause, noun phrase.**

nouns, count and noncount. A **count noun** is easily counted or divided (e.g., *tables, animals, books*). Count nouns can be plural and can be preceded by an indefinite article (**a/an**) or a definite article (**the**). **Noncount nouns,** on the other hand, are not easily counted or separated. They are often mass nouns (e.g., *cheese, butter*) or abstract nouns (e.g., *love, happiness*). Noncount nouns are never plural, and they can be preceded only by the definite article (**the**).

Some nouns can change from count (e.g., He owned two **businesses**) to noncount (e.g., He's very good at **business**) depending on the context.

It's important to know whether a noun is count or noncount so that you can choose correct quantity words. Some quantity words and phrases can be used with both count and noncount nouns (e.g., **some, any, a lot of, lots of**). Others are used only with count nouns (**many, few, several, a great number of**), and still others are used only with noncount nouns (**much, little, a great deal of, a large amount of**).

Note the errors in the following sentences:

Incorrect: I need some **advices** about finding a job.

Rewrite: I need some **advice** about finding a job. (**Advice** is noncount.)

Incorrect: Much people attended the concert.

Rewrite: Many people attended the concert. (**People** is a plural count noun.)

noun phrase. A noun phrase consists of a noun or a pronoun and all of its modifiers (if any).

In the following sentence, all of the words in boldface would be considered part of the noun phrase, which is dominated by the noun **house:**

The big, rambling, clapboard house on the hill belongs to Mrs. Adams.

See **verbal phrase, verb phrase.**

parallelism. Parallelism is the grammatical principle that words, phrases, or clauses joined in a pair or in a series must be of the same kind.

Nouns must be coupled with nouns; prepositional phrases must be coupled with prepositional phrases; adjective clauses must be coupled with adjective clauses; and so on.

Parallelism breaks down, for instance, when a noun is yoked with an adjective or when a prepositional phrase is yoked with a participial phrase. Parallelism has been preserved in the following sentence, because all the words in the series that serves as the predicate complement of the verb **was** are adjectives:

The engine was **compact, durable,** and **efficient.**

See **coordinate, coordinating conjunction.**

participle. A participle, one of the verbals, is a word that is formed from a verb but that functions as an adjective.

Because of its hybrid nature as part verb and part adjective, a participle may take an object, may be modified by an adverb or a prepositional phrase, and may modify a noun or a pronoun:

Pulling his gun quickly from his holster, the sheriff shot and wounded the murderer.

In the sentence above, the participle **pulling** takes an object (**gun**), is modified by the adverb **quickly** and by the prepositional phrase **from his holster,** and modifies the noun **sheriff.**

The **present participle** is formed by adding *-ing* to the base form of the verb: **pulling, jumping, being.**

The **past participle** is formed by adding *-ed* or *-en* to the base form of the verb or by a special spelling: **pulled, beaten, left, bought.**

The **perfect participle** is formed with **having** plus the past-participle form: **having pulled, having beaten, having left.**

The **passive participle** is formed with **having** plus **been** plus the past-participle form: **having been pulled, having been beaten, having been left.**

Adjectives can be formed from both the present participle (e.g., a **boring** movie) and the past participle forms (e.g., a **bored** student). When an adjective is formed from the past participle, it usually has a passive meaning. In the example above, it is clear that the student is bored by something. Adjectives formed from the present participle have an active meaning.

See **dangling verbal, tense, verbal phrase.**

passive verb. A passive verb is the form that a predicate verb takes when we want to indicate that the subject of the sentence is the receiver, not the doer, of the action.

The form that we use when we want to indicate that the subject is the doer of the action is called the **active verb.**

Only transitive verbs can be used in the passive form. The passive verb is made by the use of some form of the verb **to be** (e.g., **am, is, are, was, were, has been**) and the past participle of the base verb:

The shepherds **tend** the sheep. **(Active verb)**
The sheep **are tended** by the shepherds. **(Passive verb)**

See **participle, predicate verb, to be, transitive verb.**

predicate complement. Some grammarians use the term **predicate complement** to refer to any noun, pronoun, or adjective that follows, or "completes," the verb, whether it be a transitive verb, a linking verb, or the verb **to be.** Other grammarians use the term **object** for the noun or pronoun that follows a transitive verb and reserve the term **predicate complement** for the noun, pronoun, or adjective that follows a linking verb or the verb **to be.**

She is the **president.** **(Noun** following the verb to be)
She became the **breadwinner.** **(Noun** following a linking verb)

The pie tastes **good.** (**Adjective** following a linking verb)

See **complement, linking verb, to be, transitive verb.**

predicate verb. A predicate verb is the finite-verb part of the verb phrase that constitutes the whole predicate of a dependent or independent clause.

In the following sentence, the word in boldface is the predicate verb of the independent clause:

The man **guided** the dogsled through the blinding snowstorm.

See **finite verb, verb phrase.**

relative pronoun. The relative pronouns **who, which,** and **that** serve a grammatical function in an adjective clause (as subject of the clause, as object or predicate complement of the verb of the clause, or as object of a preposition in the clause) and also as the connecting link between the adjective clause and the noun or pronoun that the clause modifies.

Who is the only one of these relative pronouns that is inflected: **who** (nominative case), **whose** (possessive case), **whom** (objective case).

Who is used as a relative pronoun for people only (e.g., She's a person **who** will always tell you what she thinks). **Which** is used for animals and things (e.g., This ring, **which** is a family heirloom, belonged to my grandmother). **That** is used for both people and things (e.g., He's the one **that** introduced me to my wife. The house **that** is on your left is for sale).

Watch for these problems with relative pronouns:

Incorrect: The person that I admire **her** the most is my mother.

Rewrite: The person **that** I admire the most is my mother. (In this sentence, **that** ultimately refers to **her;** it is not necessary to repeat the pronoun.)

Incorrect: I have a friend **that her** father is a general in the military.

Rewrite: I have a friend **whose** father is in the military. (**Whose** here is a relative pronoun that replaces a possessive noun.)

See **adjective clause, antecedent, dependent clause.**

restrictive adjective clause. A restrictive adjective clause is a clause that identifies or specifies the noun or pronoun it modifies, that "restricts" the meaning to a particular person, place, thing, or idea:

My sister who just turned twenty-one went to Ireland this summer.

In this sentence, the adjective clause **who just turned twenty-one** specifies which sister went to Ireland. If that adjective clause were enclosed with commas (that is, if it were made a **nonrestrictive clause**), the sentence would mean that my only sister, who, incidentally, turned twenty-one recently, went to Ireland this summer.

A restrictive adjective clause should *not* be separated with a comma from the noun or pronoun that it modifies.

See **adjective clause, modifier, nonrestrictive adjective clause.**

run-on sentence. See **fused sentence.**

semantics. Semantics is the branch of linguistics that deals with the study of the meanings of words. As explained in the headnote to the grammar section of the handbook, in order to make sense of any language, we must know the meanings of individual words (semantics) and the grammar of that language.

sentence fragment. See **dependent clause, finite verb, independent clause.**

stem form. The stem form of the verb is the form that combines with **to** to become the infinitive: **to walk, to go.** The stem form is also the same form that a verb has when it is used with the first-person pronouns in the present tense: **I walk, we go.**

See **tense.**

subordinating conjunction. A subordinating conjunction is a word that serves as the connecting link between an adverb clause or a noun clause and a word in some other structure.

The most common subordinating conjunctions that connect an adverb clause to the verb or verbal that the clause modifies are **when, whenever, because, since, although, though, while, as, after, before, unless, until, in order that,** and **so that.**

The two subordinating conjunctions that serve as the link between the noun clause and another structure are **that** and **whether.** The conjunction **that** is often omitted when the noun clause functions as the object of a verb.

She said **[that]** the committee would not accept the proposal.

See **adverb clause, coordinating conjunction, noun clause.**

syntax. Syntax is the branch of grammar that deals with the study of how words are put together to form meaningful phrases or clauses in a particular language. Because modern English is not an inflected language like Latin, it depends mainly on word order to signal how groups of words are related to convey meaning. The phrase "the box big in" is not a meaningful unit in English. English syntax allows this arrangement of those words: "in the big box."

tense. Tense is that aspect of a verb that indicates the time of the action or state expressed in the verb. Here are the various tenses of the verb, with an indication of how they are formed:

1. **present tense**—formed with the stem form of the verb (**I run, you run**) or with *-s* added to the stem form in the third person singular (**she runs**) or with some form of the auxilary verb **to be**

and the present participle of the verb (**I am going, they are going**):

a. **simple present tense**—formed with the stem form of the verb (**I run, you run**) or with *-s* added to the stem form in the third-person singular (**she runs**).
b. **present-progressive tense**—formed with **is/are** and the present participle (verb form ending in *-ing*) (**I am running, they are running**).

The **simple present tense** describes habitual activity or unchanging states or facts (e.g., **I run every day. September has thirty days.**) The **present-progressive tense** describes a continuous action taking place right now, at this moment in time (e.g., You **are reading** this sentence. The wind **is blowing** outside right now). However, some verbs may not be used in the continuous form because they are nonaction verbs; they express a state and not an activity. Some examples of such verbs are **see, hear, be, like, need, remember, want,** and **wish.**

2. **past tense**—formed by adding *-ed* to the stem form of the verb (**walked, added**); in the case of irregular verbs, by changing the spelling (**go, went; sing, sang; speak, spoke; is, was**); or in forming the progressive tense of the verb, by using some form of the auxiliary verb **to be** and the present participle of the verb (**I was going, they were going**).

   a. **past-progressive tense**—use **was/were** and the present participle of the verb (**I was running, they were running**).

   The past-progressive tense is used to indicate that another, usually noncontinuous, action intersected with the continuous action (**I was eating** breakfast when the telephone rang).

3. **future tense**—formed with the auxiliary verb **shall** or **will** and the stem form of the verb (**You will go, we shall go**).

4. **perfect tense**—formed with the auxiliary verb **has** or **have** and the past participle of the verb (**I have walked, he has walked, they have walked**).

5. **past-perfect tense**—formed with the auxiliary verb **had** and the past participle of the verb (**you had walked, we had walked**). Use the past-perfect tense to describe an action in the past that occurred before another action in the past (e.g., **I had already eaten** dinner when you called me).

6. **future-perfect tense**—formed with the auxiliary verbs **shall have** or **will have** and the past participle of the verb (**I shall have sung, she will have sung, they will have sung**).

7. **present-perfect tense**—The present perfect is used to talk about something that happened before now, at an unspecified time, so the time words used with this tense cannot be exact.

> **Incorrect:** I **have mailed** the letter yesterday.

> **Rewrite:** I **mailed** the letter yesterday. (**Yesterday** is an exact-time word; use the past tense with exact-time words.)

Since and **for** are time words used with the present-perfect tense. Use an exact date or time with **since** (e.g., **since** January, **since** I met you), and use a period of time with **for** (e.g., **for** three weeks, **for** a century).

See **auxiliary verbs, participle, stem form.**

to be. To be is the infinitive form of the most frequently used verb in the English language, one that can be followed by a noun, a pronoun, an adjective, an adverb of place (e.g., **there, here, upstairs**), a preposition plus the object of the preposition (e.g., He is **like his father**), a verbal or verbal phrase, or a noun clause.

Here are the various forms of **to be,** as it changes in number, person, and tense: **am, is, are, was, were, shall be, will be, has been, have been, had been, shall have been, will have been.**

Some form of **to be** along with the present participle of the base verb is also used to form the progressive tense of the English verb: He **was going** to the doctor regularly. He **had been going** to the doctor regularly.

Some form of **to be** along with the past participle of the base verb is also used to form a passive verb: He **was struck** on the head. He **has been struck** on the head.

See **linking verb, predicate complement, passive verb, participle, tense.**

transitive verb. A transitive verb is a verb expressing action that terminates in, or is received by, an object.

The object of a transitive verb can be a noun or noun phrase, a pronoun, a verbal or verbal phrase, or a noun clause.

They destroyed the **village. (Noun as object)**

They shot **him. (Pronoun as object)**

She favors **giving me another chance. (Verbal phrase—here a gerund phrase—as object)**

He will try **to break the lock. (Verbal phrase—here an infinitive phrase—as object)**

She proposed **that everyone in the room be allowed to vote. (Noun clause as object)**

Only a transitive verb can be turned into a passive verb (e.g., She cooked the meal. The meal was cooked by her).

See **intransitive verb, passive verb.**

verbal. Verbal is the general name applied to participles, gerunds, and infinitives.

These words are called **verbals** because they are formed from verbs; because they are not finite verbs, they cannot by themselves serve as the predicate verb of an independent clause or a dependent clause.

See **finite verb, gerund, infinitive, participle, predicate verb.**

verbal phrase. A verbal phrase is a group of words consisting of a participle or a gerund or an infinitive and all of its complements (if any) and all of its modifiers (if any). In the following sentence, all words in boldface would be considered part of the verbal phrase, which is dominated by the participle **leaving:**

Leaving behind all of its heavy equipment, the army pressed forward quickly.

verb phrase. A verb phrase is a group of words consisting of a verb and all of its auxiliaries (if any), all of its complements (if any), and all of its modifiers (if any).

In the following sentence, all words in boldface would be considered part of the verb phrase (a structure dominated by the verb):

The army **has been severely restricted in its operations.**

See **auxiliary verb, complement, modifier, noun phrase, predicate verb, verbal phrase.**

voice. Voice is that aspect of a verb that shows the relation of a subject to the action; that is, whether the subject is the performer or the receiver of the action indicated in the verb. The former is called the **active voice** (I loved her) because the subject *I* is the performer of the action of loving; the latter is called the **passive voice** (I was loved) because the subject *I* is the receiver of the action of loving.

See **passive verb.**

word order. The order in which words appear in an English sentence is very important.

Adjective word order. Generally speaking, when you have more than one adjective modifying a noun, follow this order: amount (a **few**); descriptor (**pretty**); size (**tiny**); shape (**square**); age (**old**); color (**red**); origin (**European**); material (**wooden**); qualifier (**definite**) noun (**books**).

Inverted word order is question word order. Use inverted word order after "negative" adverbs at the beginning of a sentence for emphasis (Rarely **do I visit** my hometown); after **not only** (Not only **do I have** a cold, but I also have a fever); and with **so** as a tag (He loves golf, and **so do I**).

Adverb word order. Adverbs can be placed in a number of positions in a sentence: at the beginning (**Last month,** he moved away); in the middle (He moved **quickly** out of his house); and at the end (He moved away **last month**). Do not position an adverb between the verb and its object:

Incorrect: He moved **quickly** his furniture from the house.

Rewrite: He moved the furniture **quickly** from the house.

Commonly Misspelled Words

accept (cf. except)
accidentally
accommodate
acquaintance
acquire
address
all right
already (cf. all ready)
argument
arithmetic
athletics
attendance

beginning
believe
benign
business

cemetery
changeable
chief
choose (cf. chose)
conscious
correspondent

definite
dependent
design
devise (cf. device)
diminution
disappearance
dispel

effect (cf. affect)
embarrass
environment
exaggerate
existence

familiar
fascinate
flagrant
foreign
forth (cf. fourth)
fulfill *or* fulfil

government

harass
height
hindrance

incredible
independent
irresistible
its (cf. it's)

judgment

library
literature
lose (cf. loose)

maintenance
  (cf. maintain)
mathematics
minuscule
miracle
miscellaneous
mischief

necessary
neighbor
noticeable
nuisance

occasion
occurred
occurrence
offered

omitted

parallel
peculiar
possess
preceding
  (cf. proceeding)
prejudice
principal (cf. principle)
privilege

quite (cf. quiet)

receive
referring
relieve
remuneration
resemblance
reverence
ridiculous

seize
separate
similar
special
stationary (immobile)
stationery (paper)
succeed

than (cf. then)
their (cf. there)
threshold
too (cf. to, two)
tragedy
truly

usually

whose (cf. who's)
withhold

Index

Legend   1

Format of Manuscript 1–7 (p. 3)

Clear, Effective Paragraphs 8–10 (pp. 4–17)

Grammatical Sentences 11–20 (pp. 18–54)

Stylistic Choices: Sentences and Words 21–32 (pp. 55–99)

Punctuation and Mechanics 33–55 (pp. 100–157)